SUE HODGE

Mimi's Memoirs

A Hilarious Journey through the BBC TV'S hit comedy series 'ALLO 'ALLO

Published by Pocket Dynamo Press

First published in Great Britain in 2017 by Pocket Dynamo Press © Sue Hodge

The right of Sue Hodge to be identified as the Author of this work has been asserted in accordance with the Copyright, Designs and Patents Act 1988

ISBN 978-1-5272-0791-2

A catalogue record for this book is available from the British Library

'Allo Tony

Sue Hodge

This book is dedicated to June and Brian Hanson for their continued love and support, and in loving memory of David Croft OBE (1922-2011)

RIP Gorden Kaye (1941-2017)

It is with great sadness that in the final stages of writing this book, the country mourned the loss of a treasured friend and colleague, the great actor Gorden Kaye—known to you all as René Artois but personally known to me as 'Geordie'.
(Sue Hodge)

CONTENTS

ILLUSTRATIONS

Foreword
with Richard E. Grant

When recently speaking to Richard, we reminisced about those wonderful days with The New Shakespeare Company at the Open Air Theatre in Regent's Park. I promised I would *never* `spill the beans` about the time I emptied a pot of white powder on his head, or ripped the moustache off his face in one split second after he had carefully applied it. Therefore I won't, but when I told him about *Mimi's Memoirs* I did ask him if he had anything to add that he particularly remembered:

'When Sue and I worked together, *Time Out* Magazine described my performance as more wooden than the surrounding Regents Park trees, and I will always covet the inscribed plank 'Award' given to me by Sue Hodge and the company, whilst she rightly received rave reviews for her gigantic performance in the tiny role of Peaseblossom.'

I screamed with laughter when Richard reminded me of this and I'm grateful for his generous quote for *Mimi's Memoirs*. Upon thanking him, Richard simply replied, "My pleasure!"

With Regent's Park trees still in my mind, I remember asking Richard, 'So does the E in your name stand for "Elm"?'

Dear Richard, it is absolutely my pleasure that you took me back down that hilarious shared trip of memory lane, remembering our fun together. Thank you!

Sue Hodge and
Richard E. Grant

MIMI AND ME

I made my first professional debut in 1973 in *Jack and the Beanstalk* at The Cliffs Pavilion, Westcliffe-on-Sea, Essex, which, coincidentally is where I first met Chris Gidney in 1998 while playing Ugly Sisters with Bella Emberg in *Cinderella*. At that time I had no idea that later on Chris would play a larger role in my life.

In 1986 when Richard E Grant, Ralph Fiennes and I were giving our all for The New Shakespeare Company at the Open Air Theatre Regent's Park, none of us expected Grant to become a big film star, starting with *Withnail & I*, Fiennes to end up as Voldemort in *Harry Potter* and M in James Bond and yours truly to have made one of the biggest comedy classics ever, eventually to be seen in over 80 countries worldwide. But truth has proved stranger than fiction.

The *Daily Telegraph* had reviewed: 'This year *A Midsummer Night's Dream* is Peaseblossom'. Although the rave reviews usually go to the person playing Bottom which in 1986 was played by the much-loved Bernard Bresslaw, the *Telegraph* had decided that no role was too small and this had been proven by none other than the diminutive person about to become Mimi Labonq.

The truism of being in the right place at the right time was just about to change my career the night David Croft came to see a performance of *A Midsummer Night's Dream* with his wife Anne. 'Who's the kid?' he asked. . Anne replied she did not know. David said, 'I am going to make it my business to find out!!' Which is exactly what he did.

At that time I had no idea I would be visiting David at his house on the back of Regent's Park the following February. I arrived for the meeting; David Croft introduced himself and his co-writer Jeremy Lloyd, who promptly asked me if I could manage a French accent. I replied that the piece I was doing at the moment required a Geordie accent for which I had just been highly acclaimed. 'I think the French accent would be achievable standing on my head!' I said. They were highly amused and told me I was to be written into a program called *'Allo 'Allo*. If I found all terms acceptable it would be put through the BBC today and I would remain with them from this day until 1992. With that they bid me farewell, with thirty episodes of script under my arm to get on with for the time being.

By the end of that year Mimi Labonq was alive and kicking and unable to walk down the street without somebody shouting out, 'Allo, Mimi!!'

I have worked in the entertainment industry for forty years but am probably best known for the character role of Mimi Labonq in the BBC television series *'Allo 'Allo* which grew to worldwide recognition and shown in over eighty countries.

In a show like this, things did not always run as smoothly as they looked, and therefore it was inevitable there were going to be one or two cock ups along the way. It was the cock-ups that inspired me to write a show and to disclose the facts and outtakes that the public never saw or knew about.

In 2015 I met up with Chris Gidney again when he asked if I would like to be part of a comedy theme cruise alongside Jeffrey Holland, John Challis and Sue Holderness that Chris was putting together and compering. While we were on the ship I talked to Chris about my script idea for a show. He said it sounded great and asked, 'What have you called it, MIMI and ME?' I smiled and replied , 'I have now.' With this new title and show Chris set about booking it for the following year. The audiences loved it; then came the next challenge from Chris. 'You need to write the book,' he said.

Well, this brings us nicely up to date, and with Chris Gidney's expert help and friendship, here we are.

Mimi's Memoirs is an affectionate read and also a truthful account of what really happened during the making of that famous show. As in any show, things did not always go to plan. Some of the hair-brained schemes devised by these larger than life characters were bound to go wrong.

So, my friends, sit back and enjoy the tales and escapades of Mimi Labonq, affectionately known as 'The Pocket Dynamo'. Happy reading!

MIMI MEETS THE FAMILY

Mimi could hardly sleep for excitement at the thought of meeting her new family tomorrow; her agent and representative Michelle of the Resistance, her new boss and landlord René Artois, his wife Edith and her new friend and working colleague, Yvette Carte Blanche.

She boarded the train for London and headed for the Theatre Royal Drury Lane where they were all going to congregate. She arrived at the box office front of house and announced herself; she was shown downstairs to the room where the press launch for the new series would take place. As she entered a room full of tables with white linen tablecloths, a buffet and drinks, Mimi noticed that the room included people with cameras and recorders, all talking nineteen to the dozen and the atmosphere was buzzing. Unnoticed she wandered around the room. She decided to go up to one of the waitresses and ask her for a cup of coffee. Dutifully the waitress obliged and Mimi took the coffee, thanked her, and went to sit quietly alone to enjoy her coffee at a table in the corner without so much as a glance from anyone.

Soon the door opened and in walked Lieutenant Gruber, the British Airmen and Officer Crabtree. Flash, flash, flash, went the cameras,

"*'Allo 'Allo,* Good Moaning" came the responses. Then, much to the delight of the photographers, in came a blonde bombshell with leopard skin legs in the guise of Helga Geerhart with Herr Flick of the Gestapo. The cameras were fighting with each other to get the first picture of them with Herr Flick shouting at them, 'You will move out of the way or you will be taken outside and shot!' to much laughter and amusement. When Yvette entered the room the whole place just erupted and the cameras went off as if someone had just announced firework night. With many more people arriving the room was getting so full it was now very difficult for Mimi, tucked away in her quiet corner, to see anything.

The noise and din by now was deafening; then suddenly came the moment they were all waiting for-- Enter René and his wife Madame Edith. By this time the room was full, with every famous face from the series including the two people behind its success, writers Jeremy Lloyd and David Croft, who were now tapping their glasses with a spoon to get everyone's attention. They thanked everyone for coming and said how pleased and delighted they both were to be embarking on a new series of *'Allo 'Allo.* Mimi who in true resistance style had so far managed to stay undiscovered, was about to have her cover blown.

One of the reporters said, 'So come on then David, who is the new café waitress going to be?' As if someone had pressed an automatic button Mimi stood up and said, 'That's me!' Her eyes widened in horror as a stampede suddenly charged towards her and all she could hear was the clicking of cameras and the distant cries of laughter from her new family.

Yvette, Mimi, Helga, Drury Lane Theatre London

MIMI MAKES HER MARK

Mimi walked through the doors of the BBC rehearsal rooms in North Acton, stood in the entrance foyer and thought, 'Now where do I go?'
She then observed a huge notice board on the wall next to the lift filled with all these titles and floor levels and room numbers-- *The Paul Daniels Magic Show*, *Three Up Two Down*, *Bread*, *Brush Strokes*, *Grange Hill*-- *'Allo 'Allo* Room 602.

Mimi got in the lift, pressed level six and watched the doors close behind her, hoping for the best. She got out of the lift and started along the corridor; as luck would have it a familiar face was now heading toward her. 'Hi,' the face said, 'I'm just nipping to the loo'. It was the unmistakable Yvette Carte Blanche; Mimi just continued in the direction from which Yvette had come. Here we are. Room 602. Mimi opened the door to a noise best likened to a gaggle of geese. There was the entire *'Allo 'Allo* gang who were required for series D, Episode 4, 1987, all talking nineteen to the dozen and shrieking with laughter as if someone had shouted, 'School's OUT'!

Mimi walked in completely unnoticed and found a quiet corner in which to plant herself. Suddenly a distinctly authoritative voice said,
"Morning everyone, alright gather round". Everybody came to the large oval table, with chairs;

and for the first time the room was almost silent, except for the sound of the door opening and Yvette walking in to say, 'Sorry David, everyone, I just nipped to the loo.' Ten o'clock on the dot, Mimi observed.

'OK,' said David, 'Now we have got a few changes and new characters this season, so let's start by saying ''Allo' and introducing ourselves. I am David Croft the Producer and Director, and one of the writers of *'Allo 'Allo.'* Then a very tall, lean, suave and sophisticated gentleman announced he was Jeremy Lloyd, the co-writer of the series.

In turn, everybody said ''Allo', announced who they were until it came to the last person, who said, ''Allo, I am Mimi Labonq.' A warm and friendly laugh helped Mimi feel right at home.

Next thing, everyone read through the script to get a feel for that episode and a rough running time to prevent an overrun; everyone knew thirty minutes an episode was required.

David Croft quipped that both Jeremy and he had laughed so much when writing this particular ep that it was currently running at approximately ninety minutes. The cast greeted this with guffaws of laughter. Such excess would undeniably ensure that only the very best and finest writing would remain. All in all this exercise including coffee break took us up to our lunch break.

We would reconvene tomorrow from the top at 10 o'clock. Everybody applauded, said 'thank you', then exploded like a rugby scrum, grabbed our belongings and shot out the door, charging toward the cowering lift that awaited its usual stampede.

The BBC rehearsal canteen was on the top floor and already full of countless faces recognizable to Mimi: David Jason, Karl Howman, Paul Daniels and Debbie McGee and the entire cast of *Bread* to name but a few. If you wanted to be reminded of school dinners this was certainly the place to be. 'Goodness me, that's Joan Collins. I wonder what she's doing here?' 'Well,' thought Mimi, 'whatever it is, she's eating her school dinner the same as everyone else.'

The following day the fun-filled rehearsal room of yesterday had a little more order and composure about it as the precision of the ep took place scene by scene with head of household René in full swing. Mimi watched and listened to every single scripted detail, spoken or acted, while awaiting her cue, Michelle of the Resistance blowing her whistle to announce her arrival. Mimi felt anxious and nervous; all eyes were upon her as she made her debut entrance.

In one of Mimi's scenes Mimi with Herr Flick of the Gestapo, Flick said to David, 'Too funny, she'll have to go!' Everyone laughed except for Mimi, who wasn't sure if he'd said it as a friendly and comforting remark or if he genuinely meant it and she might be taken outside and shot!

That rehearsal day came to a much relieved end for our newcomer, and before the gang were released that day David reminded them of their necessary preparation for tomorrow. In short this meant they should all go away and arrive at 10 o'clock SHARP tomorrow with everything shipshape and crystal clear. Why? Because Wednesday's were 'Techi' days. The technicians would arrive to see the episode in full run in order to prepare everything needed for the recording in front of the live audience on Friday night.

Mimi found out from a fellow cast member, 'God help you if the techi's don't laugh at something meant to be particularly funny', as this was presumed an omen: if the techi's don't find it funny, it is unlikely that anyone else will; therefore consider it on the cutting room floor and gone from that episode. 'Gosh.' thought Mimi, 'this comedy stuff gets less funny every day.'

Room 602 was full of more bodies and hubbub than usual on Wednesday morning and the floor was drawn out *in situ* for all to see how it was going to work on set in the studio on Friday. 'I see,' thought Mimi, 'so the café lives stage right, which is stage left to you as you look at it; you go across the café into the back room, then you go behind the sets into the Colonel's office upstage right and next door to Madame Fanny's bedroom, Flick's dungeon, the kitchen or whatever is required in the episode.'

David Croft welcomed everybody, then gave a few general notes and suggested we make a start. Mimi gave a confident if somewhat nervous rehearsal with her last line, 'You will never see better paintings as long as you live', before making her last exit upstairs from the café. She stood out of sight at the top of the stairs and awaited René's final line. Then everybody in the room applauded happily; it all seemed to have been well received.

Of course the proof would be in the pudding tomorrow when they all found out what was left!!! Thursdays were always about rewrites and a final chance to adjust anything before leaving room 602 at North Acton and transferring to BBC Television Centre White City, hopefully with all your lines and scenes intact. For Mimi this was the case. She took a deep breath, and with just a hint of trepidation, she prepared for her first studio day of 'Allo 'Allo , filmed in front of a live audience-- "Aaaaghhhhhh!!!"

Mimi marched up to the front desk of the BBC reception Friday morning, gave her name and the title of the series, was ticked off the list and given her dressing room key before embarking on a long journey to find it. Once inside her home for the day, she found her tiny little costume hanging in the wardrobe with a trench coat and scarf to go over her waitress outfit for the first entrance, and her mini Mimi size two shoes sitting under it. On her dressing table was a French beret and a garter for her to conceal the handgun she was going to use in this episode. She then made her way off to the makeup department to be greeted by the friendly and soon to be familiar face of Ann Rayment, head of the department (and Mimi's personal makeup artist), who before gowning her said, 'Now-- has that top of yours got to come over your head? if so I suggest you get your Mimi blouse on so as not to ruin your hair when you pull it off after we have done it'.

With that Mimi hiked all the way back to her dressing room thinking, 'I'll remember that next time'. Once back where she last left off, Mimi was put into her gown to protect the blouse, offered tea, then made up and put into costume ready to be on set to start the morning's technical rehearsal.

Lunch break was from 1.00 until 2.00; then the tech was resumed, followed by a full dress rehearsal hopefully finished by teatime, giving everyone a chance to change out of costume, and all departments time to sit down for a meal before the live recording that evening. Everyone was then called back into makeup and costume for a final check before standing by in the wings to be introduced individually by René to the studio audience.

Mimi could now hear the piano accordion being played by Howard Leader to give a French flavour and get the audience in a typically French and lively mood. Howard Leader appeared in several episodes of *'Allo 'Allo* as a German soldier and once a ticket master. He also co-presented *That's Life* with Esther Rantzen. The buzz backstage was quite electric as the atmosphere built and 'The Gang' started to 'psyche' themselves up for battle. At this point David Croft came to Mimi to say, 'Now, we are not going to introduce you to the audience before the show because they don't know your character yet and it will spoil your first entrance. Also, don't be alarmed or put off if they don't laugh and respond to you as much as the others; remember the public already know the cast, and you are new to them, so go out there and show them what you can do. Good luck.'
Mimi didn't know whether to laugh or cry.

The applause was still going strong as the gang now returned from being introduced and René went to stand in his opening position for the episode 'Good Staff are Hard to Find', introducing Mimi Labonq to commence. Everyone wished Mimi good luck. Then René started his opening gambit and Mimi knew that she was on her own.

The show was galloping apace with a wonderful response from the studio audience which Mimi observed on the screen monitor in the makeup room.

The floor manager told her she would be collected to stand by after the entrance of Valerie Vendome, one of the new interviewees for Maria's old job. Madame Sablon had entered the café, only to be told by René and Madame Edith, 'Thank you, we will let you know'. Madame Angelique Vitesse was next in line. Mimi thought she was beautiful and bound to get the job; unfortunately, so did René, and Madame Edith sent her straight back out the door. 'Oh crumbs! This is it!' gulped Mimi as Mademoiselle Valerie Vendome entered the café.

Mimi was collected, stood outside the café door behind Michelle of the Resistance, who smiled at Mimi, waited for Valerie Vendome to exit, and promptly marched through the café door. Mimi knew that on the blow of Michelle's whistle she was in. 'Well,' thought Mimi, 'One way or another any second now for better or worse will be the changing of my life.'

The whistle blew and Mimi was on stage greeted by a huge burst of laughter from the studio audience as she stood in her French beret and full length trench coat next to Michelle of the Resistance, who announced her as the new café waitress and René's bodyguard. If not for the huge blue eyes and blonde hair one could be forgiven for thinking Frank Spencer had just walked through the door.

The audience response was big enough when she entered, but the reaction she got when she announced,

'My name is Mimi Labonq' confirmed the audience's delight. Mimi was now on a roll, carefully placing every line she had as if playing a crucial game of tennis; she just kept returning every 'ball' until René's final line which in her ears sounded like, 'Game set and match.' The credits rolled with the audience clapping whooping and cheering. Mimi Labonq knew her mark was made.

THE TOAST OF PARIS

Mimi Mimi the toast of Paris

I'm sexy I'm crazy I'm hot

Oh what a treat from the moment we meet

You will fall at my feet

I'm gorgeous am I not?

Mimi Mimi more tasty than brie

I'll call round whenever you're free

You'll have a long wait

There's a queue at the gate

And guess what the answer will be

Everybody loves Mimi!

Mimi Mimi the toast of Paris

I'm special exclusive a scoop

When you request that I throw out my chest

I'll give you my best

If you've got it let it droop

Mimi Mimi it's easy to see

The gypsy in me is aflame

Then sit in the shade and I'll call the brigade

I affect everybody the same

Everybody loves Mimi

Before joining the French Resistance, Mimi in her youth trained with *The Follies Bergere.*

Mademoiselle Mimi

THE FLYING NUN

Having been brought in to work at Café René by Michelle of the Resistance to be the new waitress and René's bodyguard, it did not take long to establish that Mimi, like every other female, had the hots for him; although he found her somewhat fanatical, after a short space of time René was very happy to have her under him.

David Croft had decided to take some of the gang out to dinner one night whilst they were filming on location and upon them all arriving back at the hotel Mimi had decided it was nightcaps all around. After she had finished her nightcap she went merrily on her way upstairs to bed. However, on reaching the top of the stairs she had a sudden impulse to slide down the banister. She made a great start at the top but lost control at the bottom and fell off into a heap on the floor. David Croft, who by this time had finished his nightcap, saw Mimi in an heap on the floor. He just stepped over her and said, 'Goodnight, see you in the morning on the end of a crane'. What could he mean? thought Mimi. Oh well, no doubt she would find out tomorrow.

The next day at 5 a.m. Mimi was called into the makeup department to get ready, then into the wardrobe department to be disguised as a nun. When ready she went outside and waited for the rest of the gang to assemble. They all boarded what they called the school bus and went off to a field for the day to film on location.

When they arrived, Mimi was introduced to another 'nun', a girl about the same size as Mimi. She would be Mimi's stunt double for the scene where they were to fly off the end of a crane. Mimi hadn't seen the crane before; it was massive and was parked across the lane at the top of the road. It had an enormously long arm with a huge whacking great hook on the end. They were going to hang Mimi on this monster in order for her to be The Flying NUN!

Both Mimi and the stunt girl were put into harnesses. They were going to hook Mimi on first; she would be raised a mere few feet off the ground in order to do the close-up shots, then lowered back down again. The stunt double would then be hooked on, raised considerably higher and flown across the cornfield. What could be simpler?
Everybody was in place and waiting for Mimi to be raised four feet into the air. The director's voice boomed out, 'OK, nice and quiet everybody, nice and quiet please we are going for a take. THREE TWO ONE ACTION!' Mimi started to wave her arms frantically about and flap her legs whilst miming 'help!' expressions as if she were being flown away. She managed to turn over onto her back and wave and flap like she was doing the back- stroke. She turned back over and started

waving her arms like a bird whilst pulling expressions of horror.

Mimi flapped and pulled faces for what seemed like an age. Finally she thought that this must be enough and so she stopped. David Croft now stood up and with a huge arm gesture motioned for her to carry on. The crane driver took this to be his cue and started to raise Mimi up higher and higher. Then he started to drive down the lane. Mimi was now flying across the cornfield with the stunt double on the ground underneath.

She could see everybody drifting further and further away until finally she ended up in the next village. René's last line to camera for that episode was, 'and good staff are so difficult to find'.

'Mimi was now flying across the cornfield with the stunt double underneath.'

MIMI GOES ROUND THE BEND

Mimi was always ready, able and willing to volunteer for anything requiring danger, bravery, or in certain cases sheer madness. She once described herself 'as bold as a wolf' with René's retort being, 'or daft as a bat!'. The time Mimi went down the sewer in an ep entitled 'Down the Drain' might well qualify for a third category—'mad as a box of frogs'.

Michelle of the Resistance had arrived at the Café René disguised as a pregnant lady. The 'bump' was in fact the enigma machine hidden under her coat. The machine needed placing in a barrel and dropping down a hole into the sewer in the town square. It then required somebody to push it into the junction. Voila! Mimi volunteered herself for the job. She appeared from the cafe dressed in a diving suit. A rope was put around Mimi and she was lowered into the hole down the sewer.

When it came to pulling her back out of the sewer by the rope, the rope slipped off, and Monsieur Alfonse, instead of pulling her back out by her feet only, managed to yank off her diving suit bottoms and Mimi slipped round the bend. She was supposed to come out the other end feet first, her legs covered by the makeup department in mud, coffee and tea.

She remembered David Croft whispering to someone who was on location watching at the time, 'Aaahhh she's a good kid, she'll do anything you want her to do'. What a lovely thing to say, Mimi thought, as she gazed down and saw the state she was in!

A rope is put round Mimi as she is lowered down the sewer

MIMI'S MAKEOVER

Great care and attention goes into the making of any period piece; this includes wardrobe and make-up whose job it is to ensure that everything is a perfect replica of the time.

When Mimi first came into the series her own hair was very long and blonde. It was decided the colour was a good contrast to that of Yvette's dark hair; Mimi's hair was, however, too long for the perfect French style they had in mind for her so it was cut to shoulder length. Mimi retained that image until an episode entitled *A Marriage of Inconvenience* was to make a drastic change to her appearance.

In this episode Madam Edith is in the back room with René and Madam Fanny is serving them dinner while Edith is reminiscing about their wedding night. The café is closed for the night so the two waitresses Mimi and Yvette have gone out on the streets as women of the night to see if they can earn a little extra pocket money. Business is not very good and they fail even to pick up Captain Alberto Bertorelli.

Both Mimi and Yvette were called in to have a meeting with the costume designer Christian Dyall for this episode. He talked through some of the ideas he thought would be suitable and also a bit of fun for this particular scene. Yvette, he had thought would be 'a scarlet woman' dressed vibrantly in red; Mimi would appear somewhat more inexperienced than Yvette, yet quite dynamic in electric blue. Everything being agreed, they left Christian and awaited the finished results.

When the time came for their final fittings, Mimi discovered that Yvette had also managed to procure a beautiful hat made of red roses to be placed strategically and stylishly on the side of her head. Mimi was to sport a glittery hair slide.

Mimi had a fabulous make-up designer at the BBC, the very experienced and much loved Anne Rayment. Mimi was in makeup discussing with Anne what they would do to make her look a bit more tarty than usual for this scene. Anne asked about Mimi's costume colour. Was she wearing anything on her head? This would affect what they might do with her hair. Mimi told Anne she had a glittery hair slide. She also just happened to mention that Yvette had got this beautiful hat made of red roses and that really she wished she had got something a little more exciting than a hair slide to wear. Anne just smiled and said, 'Well let's see what we can do'.

The day finally arrived when this episode was to be shot. Mimi and Yvette dutifully donned their costumes and went into make-up.

Much to Mimi's surprise and delight, there, sitting on her dressing table was a glorious new development for her head-- The gorgeous coiffured curls that were about to become her much-loved trade mark. Anne pinned them all carefully on Mimi's head and sent her out on set to 'GO GET 'EM!!'

As she walked onto the set to a trill of wolf whistles from the crew, Mimi remembered David Croft exclaiming, 'Good grief, I wondered who that was for a minute. I wasn't sure if it was Betty Grable or Betty Boop!'.

The new Mimi had been created and everybody loved it. AND if you look very closely in that episode you can see the glittery hair slide that Anne also placed strategically in the middle of Mimi's head.

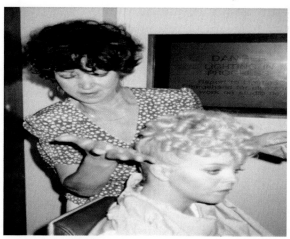

Mimi's makeover: Betty Grable or Betty Boop?

THE HUSBAND, THE WIFE, THE WEDDING.

What a joyful occasion, the day Madame Fanny married Ernest LeClerc; but Mimi nearly ended up going on their honeymoon with them.

On the day of the wedding Madame Fanny was not fit enough to make it to the altar on foot. It was decided that she should arrive at the church in her bed, the one with the famous flashing knobs. Mimi, Yvette and the two British airmen were the bridesmaids and had the job of pulling or pushing the bed. As the wedding march struck up Mimi and Yvette pulled the bed down the aisle by rope.

David Croft said, 'Now concentrate chaps because I want to do this entire scene without cutting or stopping. It is crucial that the bed hits the exact marks, in order that at the correct given moment it can be turned round on its spinning casters the other way and pulled back out up the aisle with the two airmen pulling it and Mimi and Yvette at the back pushing it .OK, nice and quiet please, we're going for a take, nice and quiet, CONCENTRATE! '

Mimi and Yvette haul the bed with all their might down the aisle. Mimi is very conscientious about its landing on the right mark. The bed comes to a stop for the scene to continue with the relevant dialogue; only Mimi can see it is a little 'off' from where it should be. The moment arrives for the bed to be spun round, but because it is not exactly in its correct place, when it is spun round it means it will be slightly off camera.

Quick as a flash and just before they spun it round, Mimi surreptitiously crossed over to the other side of the bed, pulled it onto its correct mark before giving it an almighty shove and into its correct position. Feeling mightily pleased with herself Mimi omitted to observe one thing. The wheel of the bed ran over her full length bridesmaid's dress.

The wedding march struck up, and the bed was hauled out at top speed to an enormous shriek of laughter from the congregation. Mimi, dress caught in the wheel, sank lower and lower and shrinking smaller and smaller as the castor wheel spun round and round, twisting her dress tighter and tighter until she was now on the floor being dragged along spread-eagled behind. Then, the booming voice of the director-- 'CUT!!' Which is exactly what happened, as the wardrobe department came to the rescue and cut Mimi free from the bed with no front left to her dress.

All that was left was for Mimi to look whimsically forlorn as she thought, 'Oh, what a shame. David Croft so badly wanted to do it in one take.'

**Mimi nearly ended up going on honeymoon
with them**

PRANKS IN THE PRAM

With a great comedy such as *'Allo 'Allo* and a fun loving cast it is not surprising to learn that we played a lot of pranks on each other. This particular episode was no exception when René had the last laugh on Mimi -- the episode with René dressed as a Franciscan friar and Mimi as a baby in the pram.

The first hurdle was fitting Mimi into the pram. This was handed over to the props department;, they came up with the ingenious idea of cutting a hole in the centre of the pram large enough to pass Mimi through, then making a false bottom to the underneath of the pram enabling Mimi to sit cross-legged and lie back into the top part, giving the appearance (once she was covered up) of her being small enough to fit in the pram. Once done Mimi was suitably dressed in a baby gown with beautiful matching frilly bonnet and over-sized dummy.

Such a lovely afternoon. Mimi was expecting to be pushed along the country lane in glorious sunshine by René without the distraction of Yvette or anyone else come to that matter, who would turn René's attention away from her. For once she had got him entirely to herself. They were going along their merry path with René chatting away to Mimi and Mimi belching back to him when they were stopped and questioned by a German guard as to where they were going. René explained that this baby had been left on their doorstep and he was taking it to the orphanage to be looked after. The German officer took one look in the pram; he remarked that it looked as if the baby had been left there for a very long time—and agreed to let them go.

Always at the end of any filming, the rushes are checked to ensure there is not a 'hair in the gate'--basically checking there is no debris, hair or any foreign object. A hair in the gate will remain in front of the film and create a dark line that sticks into the edge of the film frame as the camera is still filming a shot. It ruins the shot and is almost impossible to remedy after production.

René said he would go and check with the director that everything was OK and whether they could be released from this scene. He told Mimi he would push her into the shade to keep cool. Then off he went. Mimi just lay there in the pram quite contentedly and waited for him to return.

After what seemed a very long time Mimi thought she would try and get out of the pram, quite a difficult task not to tip the pram over as she had been wedged in it quite tightly. She decided against trying to get out and just shouted out to see if anyone might come.

What actually peered at her round the hood of the pram next was a cow! René had wheeled Mimi into a cowshed and for a joke had gone off and left her there. 'Blow this for a lark!' thought Mimi; she tipped the pram over and legged it out of the cowshed. Her little legs sprinted down the lane as fast as possible and back to the set, where she finally came upon René and the rest of the crew having a nice cup of tea which they spat out with laughter when they saw Mimi standing there. Chivalry? Not!

'Father' René, Franciscan au pair

Mimi—or Baby Gaga?

THERE'S NO PLACE LIKE HOME

Lynford Hall became the home base for all the gang every year when we filmed on location and turned into 'Café René. Although the cast and crew would on occasion find themselves out in a field, or a local church or a remote country lane and even Denver windmill for a day's shooting, Lynford Hall was where they were all based and affectionately known as 'Home'.

David Croft was very familiar with this place as it had already been discovered for him when filming *Dads Army.* Built between 1857-1862, the Hall was complete with formal gardens and an early Japanese water garden and designed for Stephens Lyne-Stephens, the English Tory politician who inherited a family fortune from glass manufacture and was reputed to be the richest commoner in England. In 1837 he married a French ballerina and they later bought Lynford Hall.

The Hall has entertained quite a few famous people in its time including Joe, John and Robert Kennedy. Ernest Hemingway was also a regular guest. In 1920 the Hall was struck by fire and the East wing was completely destroyed. There are still signs of the fire at the Hall today.

The government took over the Hall during World War II and it was used as a hospital.

Little did the Hall know that in time it would see the return of World War ll in the guise of a BBC television series entitled *'Allo 'Allo.*

Lynford Hall was modelled on a French Chateau, so it was very fitting for the filming of the series. The cobbled courtyard at the back of the Hall was used as the setting for Nouvion town square with Café René being erected in one of the corners. The front of the Hall was used as the chateau where the Germans had set up their headquarters. The rest of the Hall simply became a 'Haven' where the cast of *'Allo 'Allo* ran riot with their madcap antics. The Hall's new owner, Gerald F Rand, approved. He once said to Mimi, 'I always hate the day you all go home, leaving me and Lynford Hall feeling very strange and empty like the war is really over!'

Lynford Hall. Mundford Norfolk

ONCE UPON A TIME

Denise Laroque, the onetime childhood sweetheart of René, has come back to haunt him and force him to marry her. She was the leader of the Communist Resistance and, not wishing to get on the wrong side of her, René hid her and her comrade Louise upstairs in the café.

Edith, being of a slightly suspicious nature asked René if this Denise Laroque were the same girl who was his childhood sweetheart. René answered, 'No, no, no that was a different Denise Laroque.' Satisfied with this, Edith handed René a plate of sandwiches and told him to take them upstairs to her mother while she went out for a while.

Mimi knew Denise was hiding in one cupboard and Louise in another and decided also to hide from René jumping out to surprise him when he least expected it.

Initially it was scripted for Mimi to be hiding in a chest of drawers, but Mimi thought it would be funnier if she were hidden inside the grandfather clock. So the technical crew lowered her very carefully into the clock.

As René passed the first cupboard the door opened and Denise pulled him inside. She thanked him for the sandwich and after she has caressed him to bits, he stumbled out; as he passed the second cupboard, Louise threw open the door, grabbed him, pulled him in and ravished both him and the sandwiches. Louise let him out exhausted. He then passed the grandfather clock where Mimi hid. She threw open the clock door and cried, 'Rene!'-- only to be told by him, 'Not now', and he promptly shut the door shut back in her face. All went according to plan until the time came to get Mimi out of the clock. She was carefully pulled out as far as her waist to the top of the clock but as she continued to be pulled her body started to bend over from the waist leaving her legs behind. In the end her shins were grazed along the top of the clock as the rest of her emerged, bloody but unbowed to complete the episode. For once in her life, Mimi was glad her little legs weren't any longer!

Mimi thought it would be funny if she hid inside the clock

THE STAR OF THE CAFÉ

Mimi was not always part of the French Resistance, although at 4 feet 11 inches small it was easy for her to keep her ear to the ground. In her youth she had trained with the *Follies Bergere* (see p29) which now came in jolly useful for the episode where Madame Edith was indisposed.

René had told Madame Edith that Denise Laroque was out to kill her since she messed up things for the wedding, so Edith decided to flee to Spain; she went upstairs disguising herself as her mother. Mimi has decided to go and rehearse with Monsieur LeClerc; tonight she would be the star of the cabaret.

He Had To Get Under

He had to get under get out and get under
To start his little machine
A million times they'd start to hug and kiss
And then the darned old engine it would miss
And then he'd have to get under
Get out and get under
To start up his automobile.

Mimi, the star of the café

THE PATAGONIAN FRUIT BAT

One wondered sometimes if Mimi wouldn't have been better off taking up stunt work. There was her experience as The Flying Nun, and now she was going to be hung upside down outside the café door as a Patagonian fruit bat!

Herr Flick in his infinite wisdom had captured Madame Edith, Mimi and Yvette, and they were now in his dungeon being given cups of tea containing the sweat glands of the Patagonian fruit bat. This tea, according to Herr Flick, was a German phenomenon invented by Baron von Tetley containing a drug that would make them tell him the truth about the painting of *The Fallen Madonna with the Big Boobies.*

Once they finished drinking the tea, Herr Flick questioned them to check whether the tea has worked its magic. He asks them their names. Edith replies, 'Edith Melba Artois', Yvette replies, 'Yvette Carte Blanche', and Mimi sternly answers, 'Mimi Labonq!' Herr Flick was pleased with the progress of the tea so far. He then asked their respective ages. Mimi replied, '18'. Yvette replied, '19' Only when Edith replied, 'Nearly 27', that he decided the 'truth serum' tea bags were obviously a faulty batch and let the three hapless damsels return to the café.

Fortunately, the tea seemed to have no effect whatsoever, apart from the fact that Mimi was now desperate to eat fruit, kept squeaking and had a strange desire to go to sleep upside down.

David Croft asked Mimi if she was able to stand on her head; she spent many hours that day practicing headstands in order to please him. He also instructed her that, once the large bowl of fruit was strategically placed on the bar, she should be seen trying to eat as much of it as she could. Everything was set for a take. The director gave the orders, 'Nice and quiet please we are going for a take, 3,2,1, action'. Mimi spied the fruit, made a bee line straight for it and shoved the entire contents of the bowl in her face. The next thing was 'CUT! Sorry kid, we've got a technical problem.' Mimi had been 'cut off' in her prime and was now standing there with her face dripping in plums, peaches and pears and knowing just how Carmen Miranda felt!

Things were remedied, and Mimi was cleaned up and readied for her last famous mission in this episode being tied upside down to the now erected scaffolding outside the café door.

The technical crew were there to assist her climb up the scaffolding to sit on the top. They then tied a rope around her feet which in turn was tied to the top of the scaffolding bar. Mimi was sitting upright on the bar with her feet tied under it. On cue she was then going to unfold herself until completely outstretched and hanging upside down in full view. Mimi then asked René, 'Did I miss anything?' to rapturous applause.

Mimi was in her element with what she managed to accomplish but had mixed emotional memories about it. Although she felt absolutely elated, she had no way of knowing it would be the last time she would see Monsieur LeClerc. The legendary Jack Haig passed away after that episode and would sadly be with them no longer. In loving memory dear Jack.

Getting a leg over. Mimi and Monsieur LeClerc

A FISHY TALE

Having decided he cannot go on with his dangerous existence any longer, René left the café and boarded the train to Geneva. Mimi in her loyal, loving if not loony way tore off after him and boarded the train as well, as did nearly everyone else. While the train steamed along, René was forced into a situation where he had to push Mimi off the train. Mimi fell from a viaduct into the river. The train subsequently derailed and crashed, and Rene got a lift back to the café on the back of a lorry.

After a very long swim Mimi also finally made it back to the café. She burst through the café door much to the surprise of René, who never expected to see her again. They threw their arms around each other. 'Oh Mimi!' says René, 'your little heart is pounding so fast!' Only to find it was not her heart at all but a trout from the river stuck down her front.

The ill-fated trout was put into a plastic bag, slapped under Mimi's dress and onto her chest; but the problem arose when she tried to pull the trout out. She could not do it quickly enough as it kept sticking to the bag. There was also a problem for the sound man who noted that he was picking up a crackling noise from the bag as Mimi walked across the café. Consequently, the trout was taken out of the bag and wetly slapped straight onto

Mimi's chest. The longer this went on, the hotter both Mimi and the trout were getting under the studio lights, and very soon the pair of them were beginning to smell like Billingsgate Fish Market on a Saturday night. Finally everybody-- lights, camera, sound-- were happy with the scene, only to discover that the episode ran too long so the trout scene was cut. Mimi picked up a lot of trade and attracted quite a few followers that night as she was walking through the streets of Nouvion-- unfortunately they were covered in fur with whiskers, with one chat-up line--Meow!

The ill-fated train to Geneva

'ALLO 'ALLO THE HORROR SHOW

One of Mimi's favourite episodes was in series 6 and entitled *The Gestapo for the High Jump.* This episode that will be remembered for its great writers and actors; but top of the list and full marks should be awarded here to the make-up and costume department without whom this hilarious scene would not have been possible. This dream team excelled themselves here by completely changing the faces and appearances of some of the well-loved characters. Mimi was turned into a bald-headed butler with one tooth.

The butler did it!

Being of a slightly deranged character to start with, Mimi was delighted when she saw the disguise designed for her in this wacky episode. Mimi loved meeting Neil, her make-up artist for this series, every morning, watching as he deftly replaced her usual pile of curls and skilfully applied a very fine skull cap to create a bald head. Then, with careful application, Neil managed to black her teeth--all but one! Although her make-up call was around 5am to be ready on set and on location for an early start, Mimi loved the standard two hours she spent with Neil as he worked his craft to transform her into a creature befitting any production of *The Rocky Horror Show.*

**Mimi's transformation:
A bald butler with one tooth**

MIMI RUNNING FOR PRIME MINISTER

There are certain times in your life when you think, 'Yes, I Have Made It', This was certainly true for Mimi the morning she was acknowledged by everyone she passed with enormous grins on their faces and muttering witty comments.

She was used to being recognized, with people smiling and saying 'Allo 'Allo, but this particular morning seemed different. People were really laughing. It wasn't until Mimi arrived at the BBC rehearsal room in East Acton and met up with the gang that all became clear, as some of them had seen what had happened to Mimi on television the night before.

As she entered the room she was greeted with, 'Good morning, Star.' What was this about? 'I suppose we have to bow and curtsy before we are allowed to speak to you now.' Herr Flick then said, 'You were on *Spitting Image* last night. Didn't you see it?'

Spitting Image was a hugely popular satirical puppet show on ITV featuring politicians and celebrities including Ronald Reagan and his wife Nancy, Mikhail Gorbachev and Hitler, plus prominent celebrities such as Bruce Forsythe, Paul Daniels, Billy Connolly, sports icons Lester Piggott, Frank Bruno and iconic people including members of the Royal Family --and last night, guess who was on it? Yours truly, Mimi Labonq.

Who would have thought the Cabinet desk of No 10 Downing Street was now going to feature the 4 foot 11 inch Pocket Dynamo? Not seated *at* the desk but *under it. In the tradition of caricature, she* had now been reduced to half her normal size, the creators of the show exaggerating any distinguishing features and making her visually comedic. They had created a 2 foot 6 inch puppet of Mimi, with eyes as wide as two saucers and a mass of curls on her head resembling a pedigree poodle.

There at the Cabinet desk sat Mrs. Thatcher, Norman Tebbit, John Major, Michael Heseltine, Nigel Lawson, and last but not least Dennis, the inimitable husband of Margaret Thatcher., Apparently 'Order, order!' did not have quite the same meaning as usual in that episode. No, 'Order, order!', was now the cue for the Pocket Dynamo to appear to take the Cabinet's drinks orders. Mimi dutifully flew round the table taking orders, then shot off, returning with the glasses on a tray and serving them. The more she ran on and off to serve them the hotter and more frantic she got as Mrs. Thatcher's commands became more and more demanding, until eventually she looked absolutely hysterical, curls unravelling and getting longer and longer by the moment, her little legs going 19 to the dozen as she raced around the table looking like she was in training for a marathon, her face now exuding sweat and ending with fountains of water squirting out of her face and Mimi flinging their drinks at them like a Frisbee.

Apart from *'Allo 'Allo* this scene was from one of the most watched programs of its time, receiving 10 BAFTAs and two Emmy awards. Mimi had clocked up viewing figures of over 15 million people for her appearance in it, a real coup for the Pocket Dynamo.

Mimi 'ran' for the Prime Minister on Spitting Image

ONE EXTRA TOO MANY

Can you imagine being told you are going to make 26 consecutive episodes? That was the news delivered to us all one morning. Another new piece of information: our 'village' of Nouvion was moving and a permanent set would be built at the Elstree Studios, next door to the *Eastenders* set. This meant a farewell to working on location and to using the BBC studios. Everything in its entirety would take place at our new home in Elstree. 'Oh my goodness!' thought Mimi, 'I'm going to be living next door to Dirty Den!'

It was great fun arriving for the first time to our newly built café in the town square, and very soon we were all comfortably 'back in the saddle'. Not to mention saying 'Allo' or 'Good Moaning' to Angie and Den and other recognizable faces every day as we passed them in the corridor. We were given a full guided tour of Albert Square, and invited to pay a visit to the Queen Vic pub which was going to play an unexpected role in the not too distant future.

We always had extras coming in and out, or sitting in the café to create atmosphere. We would quite often see them dressed in period clothing and walking through the village square being authentic. After some time at our new home we found ourselves up to our old antics and playing pranks on each other in true *'Allo Allo'* tradition.

A new naughty idea was concocted by Fairfax, one of the British airmen, which was a touch of genius. Why, he surmised, did we not try and sneak into the Queen Vic pub unannounced unnoticed, and sit at the tables as if we were some of the extras? 'How brilliant!' we exclaimed, and set about our mission, making tentative enquiries with some of the Eastenders members as to when they would next be filming something in the Queen Vic, casually chatting so as not to arouse suspicion. Then planning which of us would not be required or missed from our set at that time and able to slip off without being noticed.

The tension to pull this plot off grew and became greater to us than any plot of Hitler's, and we found ourselves constantly looking over our shoulders to ensure nobody was listening-- and consequently became suspicious of *everyone*.

Finally the day arrived for us to perform our dastardly deed, with Flick and Helga going in undercover first and Mimi and co looking on to ensure all was safe before making their entrance. Seemed like a piece of cake with everyone naturally and comfortably dotted around the Queen Vic and the gang just keeping a low profile with their heads down and backs to the director or crew members reading a book or sitting with a glass in front of them having a drink and casually chatting.

We intruders were given certain instructions by the floor manager as to what was required of us when the director said 'Action'. 'OK, nice and quiet, nice and quiet on the set please.' We knew any minute now we would be rolling. 'Stand by and action!' There we were being filmed in *Eastenders*. We waited to hear the words 'and cut!' which meant we would have pulled it off.

Then came a real flurry of nerves as the floor manager slowly walked over to where Helga and a few other extras were sitting. 'Oh no,' we thought, 'she's been discovered', but much to our relief she had not. Instead, that group of extras were asked when they re-shot the scene, to leave the pub. Phew! They were just about to re-shoot the scene —here is where Helga made her fatal mistake. She asked the floor manager if they could request motivation from the director to cue them to leave the pub. The floor manager went over to speak to the director, who now became curious because normally the extras would do as they were asked without any query or questioning of the director. This time, as they stood by for the next take, the director paid particular attention to the group at the table who had been asked to leave the pub. As they went to make their exit he shouted out, 'Cut! Just a minute, don't I know you?' he said to Helga. 'You look vaguely familiar.'

Then with a wry smile he said, 'Alright, are there any more of you from *'Allo 'Allo* here?' We were all promptly frog- marched off.

After complaints to David Croft that he ought to keep a tighter rein on his cast, we were ordered up to his office--thinking we would be for the high jump now and possibly had gone a little too far this time. David said, 'Well that wasn't very clever of you was it? Fancy asking for stage direction, if you hadn't done that you would have got away with it you idiots. Now I'm left very disappointed in you.' Then, shoulders shaking with silent laughter, he sent us away.

The following day in the tabloids one of the headlines was "Allo 'Allo, look who's In The Queen Vic!' There in front of our very eyes was a shot of last night's episode of *Eastenders* with Fairfax the British airman, who never left the set, sitting in the corner of the pub. Not such an English twit after all, eh wot?

Nouvion moves to Albert Square.

Flight Lieutenant Fairfax/John D Collins.

The Queen Vic

I'M VERY BIG DOWN UNDER

'Allo 'Allo was now being watched by 23 million viewers at peak viewing BBC television on a Saturday night. This success prompted writers David Croft and Jeremy Lloyd to now write the *'Allo 'Allo* stage show.

The show made its debut with a huge UK tour, breaking box office records at every theatre it played. It also went on to play The Prince of Wales Theatre London twice. The television series was now gaining international recognition and we were asked to take the stage show much further afield.

Thus it came to pass that we were all given business class tickets to fly round the planet to New Zealand and Australia. All but Mimi and Yvette, that is. Some very excited male airline stewards spotted them arriving at the airport and the lucky two were instantly upgraded to First class. Oooooooohhhh you naughty boys!

The first stop in Australia was to play three sell- out weeks in Sydney before moving on to Brisbane, Melbourne, Adelaide, Newcastle, Canberra and Perth--all of which had people queuing up in the streets for any returns or standing room only. In fact the gang had to return to Perth again to meet record demand.

It was exactly the same tale when they arrived in New Zealand to play Auckland, Wellington and

Christchurch. However this part of the journey had an unexpected turn best described as 'ACCIDENTS DO HAPPEN'.

The stage show curtain had just come down to a standing ovation at The Opera House Theatre Wellington, New Zealand. In her elated state, Mimi had decided to go out with some friends to see a live band and let her hair down. The band were terribly good and energetic, and very shortly Mimi had joined that energy, dancing away. It was during her lively exhibition, her knee suddenly gave way and she found herself in a not too uncommon place--on the floor. With a little help from her friends she was escorted off the dance floor and bundled into a cab back to her hotel.

The following day to her horror, her knee seemed to be stuck in this twisted position. She could not bend or straighten her leg or come to that, walk. She telephoned the room of the company manager to report these details and within a very short space of time Mimi was being carted along to the local hospital where she was examined and x-rayed. Four hours later she was given a pair of crutches and told she would not be appearing in the show tonight. Disaster!
It was now time for the company manager to take serious action.

He got in touch with a legendary physiotherapist, John 'Doc' Mayhew, who treated the needs and injuries of the All Blacks rugby team (and who incidentally happened to be a huge fan of the *'Allo 'Allo* series). 'Doc' was delighted to come to the aide of Mimi Labonq. Unbeknown to anyone while this was happening to Mimi, Yvette had gone out for the day with some friends and had entered into game of 'Rounders'. While running her little legs off to hit the post with her bat, Yvette had accidently twisted her ankle in a pot-hole. She too was now in hospital having her ankle strapped up.

But the show must go on. Mimi made her usual entrance on stage that night thanks to Doc Mayhew, and a pair of crutches. Yvette also made her usual entrance with the aid of a walking stick. At one moment when they were both on stage together hobbling around, Rene stopped, took one look at them, turned to the audience and said, 'You can't get the Staff '.

THE LONDON PALLADIUM

By the time they returned from the Antipodean tour, *'Allo 'Allo* mania was rife and they were asked to play the most prestigious theatre in all the land, 'The London Palladium'.

Initially they were booked there to play for three months but the *'Allo 'Allo* stage show was now bringing in £300,000 per week (that's gross I hasten to add). This theatre had not had such success since the days of Danny Kaye.

Even members of the Royal Family came to see *'Allo 'Allo* at the Palladium and Mimi remembers the bout of nerves they all had when they arrived at the theatre that night to see the red carpet rolled out and heard the sound of the trumpet fanfare. The gang also found out that *'Allo 'Allo* was one of the late Queen Mother's favourite programs; in fact, some of you might remember there was an article in one of the tabloids reporting 'Queen Mother stops dinner for *'Allo 'Allo'*. The gang were all invited to the Park Lane Hotel after that performance to be guests of Prince Edward at one of his charity galas.

The Duke of Edinburgh then asked René, Yvette and Mimi if they would kindly attend a gala evening of his at Windsor alongside a host of celebrities including Cleo Laine and Johnnie Dankworth, who were to sing that night. As it turns out René also ended up singing that night to rapturous applause when he brought Mimi and Yvette on stage with him and gave his own rendition of 'Thank Heaven for Little Girls'.

This was not Mimi's only encounter with the Royal Family, as she and René were asked to be part of a Royal Command Performance at London's Dominion Theatre, Tottenham Court Road. They sang together that night and everybody loved them including a production company who promptly invited them to work together at Christmas for them in a production of *Peter Pan* playing Captain Hook and Smee. Mimi spent a brilliant Christmas with René that year with Mimi always having the last laugh-- René was made to walk the plank every night!

Sell-out show—Peter Pan

MIMI GOT CARRIED AWAY

Yvette and Mimi were walking along the streets of London admiring the big English city fashions when a man passing by them abruptly stopped.

'Mimi,' he said, 'OH! I love you!' With that he promptly threw her over his shoulder and ran off with her down the street. Mimi, gob- smacked, could see Yvette sitting on the curb of the pavement crying with laughter as Mimi hurtled along the street bouncing against the man's back. Naturally people stopped and stared as they heard Mimi's cries and screams as the man passed them laughing his head off and whooping for joy.

He finally returned Mimi safely back to Yvette and said, 'Sorry, I just had to do that', then left.

This stranger had achieved much more than realizing a dream come true, because for the first time in her entire life, Mimi Labonq stood there, completely and utterly SPEECHLESS!

Getting rather carried away

GOODBYE HITLER, 'ALLO GOERING

In the last scene of the *'Allo 'Allo* stage show nearly everyone ends up on stage dressed as Hitler including Mimi as a miniature Hitler. Then General von Klinkerhoffen enters to say, 'There are in this café many Hitlers'-- until David Croft came up with the ingenious idea of removing Mimi from her Hitler role and at the last minute bringing her on as the corpulent Hermann Goering, her image being as wide as she was tall. Mimi was taken to a specialized costumier to have this costume made as it had to be made from a special type of foam to: Keep its shape--

Keep its shape while being rolled across the ground--

Keep its shape while being rolled across the ground with Mimi in it.

Mimi was very excited and proud as David Croft accompanied her to the makers for her first fitting. Measurements were taken. Theory and practice were discussed. Then back they went to the BBC together and awaited the call for Mimi's second fitting.

On the return visit, Mimi found herself encased in rubber foam with her arms and legs sticking out just visible, and her head on top like the lid of a jug. David Croft roared with laughter at the sight of her, but when they laid her on the floor and tried to roll her along, the thing just collapsed as Mimi turned over and she could feel the floor through it. The makers said this foam was too thin. They would have to make it from more durable materials. 'Thank you very much,' said David. 'We will wait to hear from you.'

The next telephone call came soon and back they went. This time Mimi found herself in what can only be described as a barrel. There was no arguing with the fact that this was definitely a stronger design--so much so that it was impossible for Mimi to do anything in it. The thing was just not pliable at all. Away they went again with an unsatisfactory result. David was confident they would get there in the end.

'Here we go then,' said David, 'Third time lucky,' thought Mimi, and they were right; this time the article was bang on! Having been perfected by the makers from a specialized type of rubber foam, it now resembled a huge egg that opened down the front with a pair of powder blue trousers attached for Mimi to climb into, get her arms and legs through easily, and be zipped up to the neck with her head poking out the top--a magnificent Herman Goering jacket completed by a hat now placed perfectly upon her head. They carefully laid Mimi on the floor and successfully rolled her from one side of the room to the other. Voila!! The original 'Fatman' had been created.

Poor Mimi was so nervous that first time she stood outside the café door in it waiting for her cue because she knew if she did all the things she had rehearsed, she was capable of bringing the house down. Little did she know she was just about to bring everything else down with it. She heard her cue from Madam Edith on stage as Hitler, 'Where is Herman Goering, the head of my glorious air force?' Mimi took a deep breath and bellowed off stage at the top of her voice, 'I am here mien Führer' and with that burst through the café door. She was so fat she could hardly get through the café door.

The audience screamed with laughter at the first sight of this apparition. Delighted with the response, Mimi tried to run into the café. Unfortunately, due to the size of this thing she did not see the step down from the door into the café and missed it. In true Herman Goering style she flew through the air and landed slap bang centre stage on the floor at Hitler's feet.

The audience roared a huge boost of laughter. Although unhurt her flying entrance caused a huge problem for Mimi, on her back, on the floor and unable to get herself back onto her feet flailing her arms and legs frantically and looking like a deranged fat fly.

Captain Bertorelli rushed to her aid, grabbing her flailing arms and trying to pull her back up. He very nearly succeeded, managing to get her halfway upright, but the weight of the thing was too great, pulling him back down and on top of Mimi. They both were now frantically flapping their arms and legs about and now doubling up on the deranged fly act. The audience were howling with laughter not to mention the cast, who could not believe their eyes. René then came to the rescue, pulling Captain Bertorelli off Mimi and back onto his feet. The two of them rolled Mimi off into the wings as fast as they could, in order to get on with the scene.

Unfortunately, it did not stop there because they rolled the thing with its little person inside so fast that as it hit the wings it also hit into the rubbish bins, the company manager and the fire buckets. The audience screamed with laughter at this cacophony, but what happened next defied even Mimi's credulity. Two members of the stage crew who thought they were helping, rolled Mimi back on stage. As she rolled she smashed into the proscenium arch where she made a final landing.

General von Klinkerhoffen tried to continue with his line and through near hysteria managed in a high-pitched voice to squeak out, 'There are in this café many Hitlers'. René now throws in, 'Not to mention a half pint Herman Goering with a suspected broken back and a stage full of actors crying. By this time and goodness knows how, Mimi had managed to get herself on all fours with her head facing the front. She took one look at the audience and said, 'Ladies and gentleman I think I can safely say I have truly THROWN myself into this roll tonight. I thank you!' The audience responded with probably one of the biggest rounds of applause Mimi had ever heard.

David Croft was in the audience that night to see how the 'Fatman' went. He came backstage after the performance to Mimi's dressing room and said, 'Well love, don't make it too long, but keep it in eh!' With a big smile and a wink he made an exit.

Poster, Royal Gala Performance, 1989

VISUAL EFFECTS

There are so many elements involved in making any project successful. Importantly, so many people behind the scenes with their expertise and knowledge should be remembered, highly praised and credited because we simply could not create half of what happens without them.

Our visual effects team were among these people and were top class at their job. They became affectionately known to the gang as 'The Visi Fects Boys'.

There was nothing we enjoyed more than waiting to see the local pissoir explode, or Gruber's little tank get blown up, or the door to Herr Flick's dungeon blown off enabling von Smallhausen's line 'I forgot my key' to be doubly funny when he entered. All ideas created and brilliantly written of course, by Croft and Lloyd.

The Jet Propelled Mother in law was absolutely hilarious the day smoke and fumes were seen pouring out the back of Madame Fanny's wheelchair and it went whizzing off with her still in it as she was just about to sample a glass of wine. Then there was the day Officer Crabtree had gone in to use the local town square convenience and it was hit by a tank, leaving him not only relieved but also as flat as a pancake as the tank continued going.

The props department also came into their own here, as the two dummies of Madame Fanny and Officer Crabtree were made with incredible verisimilitude and brilliantly staged by the 'Visi Fects Boys' We never saw the switch when brilliantly edited on the cutting room floor. No doubt about it-- a first class creative team is essential and worth its weight in gold.

One of Mimi's favourite effects times was on *The Train to Geneva.* Not only was this another episode where their team skills were called for, but on this particular occasion they appeared to be in the episode as well.

René has nicked a fortune in gold and was sick to the back teeth of the war, Michelle of the Resistance and of his wife, not necessarily in that particular order. René left the café and boarded the train for Geneva, thinking of Yvette. It happened that nearly the entire cast for one reason or another also ended up on that train.

A beautiful steam train was filmed arriving on location with the cast required on the station. However, the scenes shot inside the train were a more technical matter and the railway carriages were erected in the studio. A huge number of enormous tyres were placed in a long line, then piled up a few feet high with the railway carriages carefully positioned on top of them.

This very peculiar looking image met us when we were called in to rehearse the interior shots; on the other hand, not half as peculiar looking as what we were about to witness.

Before we boarded the carriage to begin the scene, we met with the director Richard Boden, who said, 'Now don't forget you are on a train and that the train is in motion; all your movements will need to be a little off balance so as you proceed along the carriages don't forget to stagger a bit or fall into the side of the carriage or even lean on the windows to steady yourself. At all times remember the rhythm of the train, *da ga da dah, da ga da dah, da ga da dah.*' This was going to be great fun to shoot we thought.

Up came Mimi's scene. Already costumed and made up, she dutifully boarded the carriage. She was used to seeing the boom operator holding the microphone over and above her head and the cameraman in front of her, but what she was not used to seeing was the 'Visi Fects Boys' standing in what looked to be like the shot as well. Mimi could hardly contain herself let alone speak, when she heard, 'Action!'. The 'Visi Fects Boys' starting rocking from side to side, transferring their weight from one foot to the other whilst travelling backwards to give the effect of the motion of the train as Mimi was supposed to be travelling forwards.

Mimi, however, did not travel forward; instead she travelled downwards and ended up a hysterical heap on the floor speaking her new impromptu lines, 'Oh my God, oh my God, I'm so sorry, I'm so sorry!' topped off with an enormous snorting piggy laugh. 'Cut!' came the command. By now everyone was helpless with laughter. The director came into eyeshot and said, 'OK OK, maybe I should have said beforehand that the guys have been put on board to enhance the rolling motion of the train, which is why the carriages are on this pile of tyres to enable them to rock gently from side to side. I thought it would surprise you.' Mimi replied, 'surprised me? It nearly killed me.' Then a real shock horror moment filled her as she thought, 'Oh no, I've got to do that again!' She was right. She did have to do it again but not before returning back to makeup.

Bound for Geneva

New Kid on the Block

Introducing Mimi Labonq – ooh la la !

The Poodle Parlour

The Gang

'My Name is Mimi Labonq'
Do not mess with moi!

Ohh Rene'!

Little French Riding Hood

Yvette and Mimi: 'Stick 'em Up!'

Two Little Maids from School

Why am I Always the Bridesmaid?

A Solemn Undertaking

Mimi the German Chauffeur

The Nouvion Oars

Yvette, Edith, Mimi
Ooh La La Encore!

Legs Eleven

The Dark Side

Original Studio Ticket

Location Location!

'I'll Have a Threepenny One Please'

Wide Eyed and Legless

So Angelic

And of Course!
The Fallen Madonna with the Big Boobies

MIMI'S ITALIAN JOKES

Have you heard about the new Italian tyres?
Dago round Dago through mud Dago through snow
Dago everywhere and when they go flat Dago Wop
Wop Wop Wop!

Mimi sat in the police station crying, 'I've been seduced
by an Italian.'
The Gendarme, 'How do you know he was Italian?'
Mimi, **'Because I had to help him!'**

Q: What's red green purple blue yellow and orange?
A: **Captain Bertorelli dressed up!**

Q: What happened to the Italian chef that died?
A: **He pasta way.**

Q: Where do pepperonis go on holiday?
A: **The leaning tower of pizza!**

Knock Knock. **Who's there?**
Snow. **Snow who?**
Snow laughing matter.
**You Can Say That Again! What a Mistake-a to
Make-a!**

MIMI TRANSLATES CRABTREE

Moo Moo
Mimi

Ronnie are you aloon?
René, are you alone?

That is a fanny name
That is a funny name

I was pissing your coffee
I was passing your café

It was a very dick night
It was a very dark night

I saw two men leaking at your dustbins
I saw two men looking at your dustbins

Ronnie can you drip your bum?
Rene can you drop your bomb?

Hole Hotler!
Heil Hitler !

Follow that nin
Follow that nun

Farty fighting bummers
Forty fighting bombers

Herr Flock of the Gestoopo
Herr Flick of the Gestapo

Hello Wombledon sox sox sox
Hello Wimbledon six six six

Up the crook without a piddle
Up the creek without a paddle

I was passing by the door
I was pissing by the door

When I heard two shats
When I heard two shots

We wee too much
We weigh too much

It has cripped on your hod
It has crapped on your head

Would you lick Ronnie out of the wee
Would you like Renè out of the way?

Diffodils and doses
Daffodils and roses

I have my dirty to do
I have my duty to do

Ribbing the bonk
Robbing the bank

Mimi and Crabtree
Small is Beautiful- and Cute-i-Ful

MIMI'S WARTIME MENUS
MIMI'S MINI DUMPLINGS

INGREDIENTS
4 oz plain flour
1 dessertspoon (2 tsp) baking powder
1 tsp castor sugar
1/2 tsp salt
1/2 oz butter
4 fl oz milk

Method. Pre-heat oven 200° C, 400° F
Stir together flour, baking powder sugar & salt
Rub in butter until crumbly
Stir in milk to make a soft dough
Drop by spoonfuls into your favourite boiling stew
Cover and simmer for 15 minutes
C'EST TRES BIEN!

RENÉ'S ROASTED RISSOLES

INGREDIENTS
8 oz minced beef
1 onion
1 small carrot
1 egg
3/4 cup breadcrumbs
Worcestershire, tomato & bbq sauce
Minced garlic to taste

Method
Heat oven 200 °C, 400°F
Put mince in a bowl.
Finely dice onion and add.
Crack the egg into bowl.
Add breadcrumbs and garlic.
A dash of all 3 sauces.
Hand mix it all together
Cover a shallow baking tray with foil
Roll the mixture into balls
Place in oven for 50 minutes
BON APPETIT!

CRABTREE'S CRUNCHY CRABCAKES

INGREDIENTS
One inch piece fresh peeled ginger, finely chopped
2 red chillies (remove seeds)
9 oz white crabmeat
1 Tbsp fresh chopped coriander
2 spring onions finely sliced
2 eggs
7-8 Tbsp breadcrumbs
Plain flour to dust
1 fl oz olive oil

Method—Pre-heat oven 180°C, 350°F
Pulse and finely chop ginger and chilli in a blender.
Combine in a bowl with the crabmeat, coriander and spring onion.
Crack in one egg and mix.
Stir in 4 tablespoons breadcrumbs.
Divide mixture into 6 equal parts.
Place moulded cakes onto a tray.
Chill in fridge 20 minutes before cooking.
Beat the remaining egg in a small bowl with a tablespoon of water.

Place some plain flour and remaining breadcrumbs in a shallow dish.
Dredge a crab cake in the flour then dip into egg mix.
Heat oil in a frying pan.
Gently fry crab cakes 2-3 mins each side
Transfer onto a baking tray
Bake 5-10 minutes.
Can be served with a sweet chilli jam
BON GOUT!

YVETTE'S BUN IN THE OVEN

INGREDIENTS
1 tablespoon active-dry yeast
½ cup warm water
½ cup milk
1 large egg
2 Tbsp vegetable oil
2 Tbsp sugar
1 tsp salt
3 cups all purpose flour
1 Tbsp butter

Method—Pre-heat oven 190°C, 375°F
Put yeast into bowl and stir in the water.
In a separate bowl whisk together milk egg oil sugar salt.
Add this to the yeast mixture and stir until combined.
Add all the flour and stir until it forms a dough.
Knead the dough for 10 minutes.
Place in bowl and cover.
Let dough rise in a warm spot until double its original size (approx 1 hour).
Sprinkle flour onto work surface.
Place dough on top.
Divide into 12 pieces.
Shape into buns.

Arrange on non-stick pan let them rise (30-40 mins).
Brush rolls with melted butter
Bake rolls until golden (15-18 mins).
Lift rolls from pan and cool on wire rack
MANGER SI VOUS PLAIT!

HELGA'S CHEESY RAREBIT

INGREDIENTS
8 oz grated cheese
1 Tbsp butter
2 tsp Worcestershire sauce
1 tsp dried mustard
2 tsp flour
Seasoning of pepper
4 Tbsp beer
Sliced bread

Method
Melt the butter in a pan.
Add grated cheese stir over low heat until melted.
Pour in the ale.
Add mustard and any seasoning.
Bring mixture to boil and remove from heat.
Toast the bread.
Place bread on baking sheet; pour over the mixture
Grill, or very hot oven (225° C, 450°until golden
VOILA!

FANNY'S FLAPJACKS

INGREDIENTS
6 oz butter or margarine
6 oz dark brown sugar
6 oz golden syrup
12 oz rolled oats
1 ½ oz raisins or sultanas

Method – Pre-heat oven 180 °C, 350° F
In a saucepan over a low heat combine the butter sugar and syrup.
Cook stirring occasionally until butter has melted.
Stir in the oats and sultanas until coated.
Pour into an 8 inch sq or 20 cm sq baking tin.
Bake for 30-40 mins until brown.
Remove from oven and cut into squares.
FABULEUX!

GRUBER'S LITTLE GINGERBREAD MEN

INGREDIENTS
3 ½ oz butter
12.4 oz plain flour
1 tsp bicarbonate soda
4 tsp ground ginger
6 oz dark brown sugar
4 Tbsp golden syrup
1 large egg, beaten
Currants to decorate

Method-- - Preheat oven 190˚C 375˚F
Grease 3 baking sheets.
Sift flour bicarbonate soda and ginger into bowl.
Rub the butter into the dry ingredients to form fine breadcrumbs.
Stir in the sugar.
Mix together the syrup and egg and pour into dry ingredients.
Bring the mixture together with a fork, then by hand and knead until smooth.
Divide the dough into three equal portions.
Roll out each to 0.2 inch thickness and cut out gingerbread shapes.
Lift the gingerbread men onto baking sheet.
Make faces with the currants.
Bake for 15 mins
PERFEKT!

VON KLINKERHOFFEN: THE PERFECT SAUERKRAUT

INGREDIENTS
5 lbs green cabbage, shredded
2 tsp caraway seeds
1 quart water in a sanitized glass jar
3 Tbsp pickling salt
1 Tbsp juniper berries

Method
In a large mixing bowl mix cabbage thoroughly with salt juniper berries and caraway seeds. Let stand for 10 mins.

Pack cabbage mixture down into a large plastic food container. Top with a lid smaller than the opening of the container and place a glass jar filled with the quart of water on top of the lid. Place in cool area overnight (21°C 70°F).

Check cabbage every other day for two weeks and skim the surface of scum if necessary. Let stand for four weeks then transfer to an airtight container and store in the fridge for up to 6 months.

DAS BESTE!

COLONEL'S COCK A LEEKIE

INGREDIENTS
1 whole chicken with giblets
2 bay leaves
500g of leeks chopped, white/green parts separated
2.5 litres water
30g rice
Salt/ Pepper to taste

Method
Place the chicken bay leaves green parts of the leeks and water in a large stock pot. Bring to the boil then reduce heat to a simmer. Simmer gently, covered, for 3-4 hours.

Remove chicken, giblets, and bay leaves from pot. Skim fat from surface of the stock.

Add rice white part of the leeks, salt and pepper to the stock. Simmer vigorously for 15 minutes until rice is tender.

Shred desired amount of chicken meat and add to the pot.

Reserve the remaining chicken for another use.

Simmer a further 5mins.

WUNDERBAR!

VON VIENNA: SMALL SCHNITZEL HAUSEN

INGREDIENTS
1 quart of oil for frying
6 6oz fillets pork sirloin
1 cup cake flour
2 cups dry breadcrumbs
2 eggs
¼ cup milk
Salt/Pepper seasoning

Method – Heat deep fryer to 180°C 350°F

Place meat on solid surface and pound with mallet to quarter inch thick.

Place flour and breadcrumbs in separate dishes. Lightly beat egg and add milk. Season and put into another dish.

Coat the meat in flour, then dip in into egg mixture. Coat with breadcrumbs then deep fry in the oil until golden brown.

ZERTRUMMERUNG!

FLICK'S FLEISCHKUEKLE

INGREDIENTS
For the Dough:
3 cups flour
1 tsp salt
Equal amounts water/cream to make the dough
For the Filling:
2 cups ground beef
1 cup chopped onion
Half cup water
Salt/Pepper seasoning

Method
Roll out the dough to the size of a saucer. Mix the filling together and put onto half the side of the dough. Fold the dough over and seal the edges. Deep fry until golden brown.
YOU WILL ENJOY THIS OR YOU WILL BE SHOT!

MONSIEUR LECLERC'S ECLAIRS

INGREDIENTS
4 Tbsp whole milk
4 Tbsp water
50g/2oz unsalted butter
1 tsp castor sugar
Pinch salt
100g /4oz flour
4 medium eggs, beaten

For the Filling:
20g /3/4 oz oz unsweetened chocolate
450g/1lb pastry cream (cream patisserie)
1 Tbsp sifted cocoa powder

For the Glaze:
200g/7oz white fondant icing
1 Tbsp cocoa powder
1-2 tsp water

Method - Preheat oven 170°C 325° F
1. For the choux pastry place the water, milk, butter, sugar, salt in a medium saucepan over a high heat and bring the mixture to boil.
2. Remove the pan from the heat and using a wooden spoon quickly beat in the flour until the mixture is smooth.

3. Turn the heat down to medium return the pan and cook for 1min beating all the time until the mixture comes away from the edge of the pan

4. Remove the pan from the heat and gradually beat in the eggs until you have a smooth dropping consistency. It may not require all the egg

5. Transfer the paste to a large piping bag fitted with a 1.5cm half inch nozzle and let the mixture cool for 5mins in the bag to stiffen.

6. Line a large baking tray with greaseproof paper and pipe on 12 éclairs approx 15cm/6in long

7. Bake the éclairs in the preheated oven for 30-35 mins then transfer to a rack to cool

8. For the filling, melt the chocolate in a bowl over a pan of simmering water. Pour the melted chocolate into the pastry cream, mix in the cocoa powder and whisk together until smooth.

9. Transfer the filling to a piping bag (0.5cm 1/4 inch fluted nozzle). Pierce the underside of each éclair four times with the tip of the nozzle, gently squeezing a little into the éclair.

10. For the glaze, gently warm the fondant in a small pan over a light heat until it reaches body temperature.
Stir in the cocoa powder and enough water to make a paste, then transfer to a piping bag fitted with a 1 1/2cm ½ inch nozzle.
Pipe the glaze onto the top of each éclair, then place in the fridge for the glaze to set.
UNE TOUCHE D'ARTISAN!

VEGETABLES ALFONSE A LA GRECQUE

INGREDIENTS
¼ cup plus 2 Tbsp extra virgin oil
½ cup dry white wine
½ cup water
¼ cup white wine vinegar
1 tsp coriander seeds
3 bay leaves
½ tsp black peppercorns
½ tsp fennel seeds
½ tsp dried thyme
Salt
1lb carrots peeled and cut
1 ½ pounds medium onions cut into eighths
12 oz small white mushrooms quartered
Freshly ground pepper

Method
In a large deep skillet combine half cup of the oil with the wine, water, vinegar, coriander seeds, bay leaves, peppercorns, fennel, thyme and 1 tsp of salt. Bring to the boil over a high heat. Add the carrots. Cover and simmer over a moderate heat stirring occasionally until the carrots are barely tender. Add the onions and mushrooms, cover and simmer stirring occasionally until the onions are crisp tender.

Transfer the veg into a bowl and let cool. Stir in the remaining 2 Tbsp of olive oil and season with the salt/pepper.

Remove the bay leaves and peppercorns before serving. **EXTRAORDINAIRE!**

MADAM EDITH'S TWICE COOKED DUCK

INGREDIENTS
Oil to cook
2 Tbsp minced garlic
2 Tbsp minced ginger
1 Tbsp fermented black beans
¼ cup chopped scallions
1/2 cup hoisin sauce
1 cup red wine
1 cup dark soy sauce
½ cup sugar
1 whole duck

NOTE You can either purchase a ready cooked duck or roast in the oven 180°C 350°F for 1 hour (30 mins each side).

Method
In a large sauté pan coated with oil, sauté on medium the garlic, ginger, black beans, and scallions until soft. Add hoisin and stir for 2 mins. Add the red wine soy sauce and sugar. Bring sauce to boil then add roasted duck. Turn duck frequently to completely coat with sauce for 15 mins then remove duck. Keep sauce on a low simmer Break down duck into small pieces and add back to the sauce completely coating. Then serve.
ABSOLUMENT QUACKING!

JUST ONE CORNETTO
(Alberto's Homemade Italian ice cream)

INGREDIENTS
300ml (1 1/3 cup) cream
500ml (2 cups) milk
8-10 egg yolks
150-175ml (1/2-3/4 cup) sugar
1 vanilla bean

Method
Combine the milk the vanilla bean (split lengthways) and half of the sugar in a saucepan.

Heat on medium-low to just below boiling point, remove the pan from the heat and set aside for 20 mins to allow the vanilla flavour to infuse.

In another pan combine the egg yolks with the remaining sugar and whip the mixture for a couple of minutes. Take the vanilla infused milk, and bring it back to the heat. Before the milk begins to boil pour some of it onto the egg yolk/sugar mixture in a thin stream while whisking steadily. This little by little approach is supposed to temper the eggs making the yolks less likely to transform into scrambled eggs when confronted with the milk.

After the tempering has been done the rest of the milk/cream is added to the yolk mixture. Then on a medium-low heat while stirring constantly bring the ice cream base up to 85°C 185°F.

Remove from heat and allow to cool.

When cool enough for the refrigerator the ice cream base should be covered and left to mature over night, leaving the vanilla pod in. After this the vanilla pod can be taken out, the vanilla seeds scraped back into the base, which then can be poured into an ice-cream machine and frozen.

DELIZIOSO Just like mama used to make!

MIMI'S MEMORABLE MAIL

You would not believe the amount of fan mail Mimi has received and responded to over many years, and how many signed photographs have been sent out both in the UK and all over the world. The fan base in Europe is enormous as it is also in the Antipodes. Many thousands of letters have come from children of all ages, and perhaps controversially there have been quite a few letters and interest from death row.

Mimi has sent photographs, memorabilia and any help she has been able to give in answer to more charities than she can remember and an incredible number of signed Christmas cards and birthday wishes responding to so many of the lovely letters that say, 'my son (or) my daughter is a huge fan of the program and Mimi is their favourite character; it would be a wonderful surprise if you could sign this card and wish them a happy birthday, (or) a happy Christmas'.

The praise and generosity from the fans over the years has been endless with letters saying, 'This is some of the funniest comedy ever'. They also talk about the catchphrases saying, 'Listen very carefully I shall say this only once, was the funniest line in the show (or), my family still say Good Moaning to each other every morning.' One fan said he loves being able to say to his wife, 'You stupid woman' and gets away with it now because René always does. One of Mimi's particular favourites said, 'This show is divine, so many great characters with so many great things about them. How they filmed this with a straight face I'll never know. This is the zenith of farce comedy, David Croft has to be one of the greatest British comedy writers ever'.

There was a lovely one-off fan letter: 'Listen very carefully I shall say Zis only once. Guten Tag, 'Allo 'Allo'

The other day a beautiful letter arrived saying, 'Thank you for so much pleasure fun and laughter you gave to my 94 year old mother who has just passed away; she treasured your signed photo and was still laughing at your programme right up until the day she died'. No two letters are the same and they come from all walks of life and people of all age groups and nationalities.

One occasion Mimi will never forget is the time her London agent telephoned to ask, 'Have you got any relatives in New Zealand, only three enormous wrapped items have arrived here at my office from overseas, they are sent from a family of the name Wiltshire. They are the size and shape of what can only be described as three coffins, large, medium and small. They weigh a ton and are blocking up the entire entrance to the office, and it has been suggested by the staff on reception that the police be informed of these peculiar suspicious objects. What do you want me to do about this?' Somewhat concerned as Mimi knew she didn't have any relatives in New Zealand where the enormous objects had been sent from and certainly did not wish the police to become involved or cause any further trouble to her London agent, she decided to get them couriered to her own address right there and then. The parcels arrived later that same day. Mimi opened the door to a man who said, 'Is there anybody who can help me in with these?' He opened the back of his van and just as the agent had said, three enormous coffin-shaped wrapped boxes appeared. Mimi and the man staggered beneath the weight of each one out of the van and inside the house. 'Sign here', he said, and then he left.

Mimi was both curious and absolutely gobsmacked! What on earth could these be? Where to start with opening them? Knowing Mimi as you all do, no need to ask where she started -- Of course, the big one first.

On closer examination of the biggest one, she observed where it said 'SENDER: Wiltshire', that the sticker was in fact stuck over a brown envelope with a letter inside saying, 'You look a sporty outdoor girl, outdoor girls are fun. We thought you might enjoy these'.

No 1. For you and your family

No 2. For you and your partner

No 3. For you if you have no family or partner

The plot thickened. Then Mimi saw that they were all numbered. Right. Here goes number one first. For the next half hour Mimi felt like her Birthday, Easter, and Christmas had all come at once as she waded through a mass of paper packaging and tape. Finally it all became clear, and after discarding all the rubbish she was left standing in a pile of canvas, poles, rods and pegs in the guise of three variously sized camping tents. No 1 to sleep six people, No 2 to sleep you and a friend and No 3 all covered in pink hearts to sleep just one, should you be camping alone. Mimi sat there amongst it all in a heap of laughter as she thought, 'I wonder what the police would have thought should they have been called?'

Being only 4ft 11 inches tall and quite childlike both in stature and impish behaviour, Mimi loved one letter from an 11 year old:
Dear Mimi.
'My name is Sarah. I am 11 years old and both my brother and me love *'Allo 'Allo* and we really love Mimi and think she is a great character. We love how she is always doing dangerous things and not

afraid of anything and always trying to think up new plans. We would like to try and help. We have been thinking. Helga wears a lot of red lipstick. If you were to get hold of one of her lipsticks and inject it with poison, the next time she put it on she would poison herself and die and you would become the bravest person in all France.
Love Sarah' xxx
'P.S Would it be possible for you to send a signed photo to me and my brother.'

Mimi Labonq

THE LAST SUPPER

There was a very sombre atmosphere this particular Friday when Mimi walked into the studio. She was usually one of the first to arrive as she was always one of the first to be called into makeup to be ready on set to rehearse for the first scene which nearly always took place in the café. She walked into the makeup room and there was Yvette sitting in her usual place with her dressing gown on, already having her makeup applied. 'Morning darling,' Yvette said, 'Aaahhh, isn't it sad?' Mimi nodded yes and was handed her dressing gown to put on and one of the make-up artists asked, 'Can I get anyone a tea or a coffee?' Mimi and Yvette sat side by side, staring at each other in the mirror almost in disbelief as the team continued to get them ready to rehearse the first scene on set for the very last time. The war was over today and much celebration was about to ensue, although at this moment neither Mimi or Yvette could think of much to celebrate and shout about. For them this meant *'Allo 'Allo* had finally come to an end.

They walked onto the set where they were required to mime to the Andrews Sister's record *The Boogie Woogie Bugle Boy* with Madam Edith. Normally this would have been hilarious and great fun to do but today after they had finished singing, with the interruption of René coming through the café door and turning the gramophone off to give his line, the three of them looked at René and burst into tears. René just stared at them and said, 'I haven't even said anything yet!'

The rehearsals continued for the rest of the day until it was time to break for dinner, when the gang all went to the BBC restaurant for their last supper together. They all ordered their usual choice on a Friday night, of egg and chips. This ritual had originally been started by Herr Flick of the Gestapo, who once said, 'You will all order egg and chips in the hope it will make you funny tonight.' Consequently, the meal became known as 'Comedy egg and chips'. After the meal, the gang went back into make-up to get patched up and then off to their dressing rooms to be put into costume by the wardrobe department. Once they were ready, they came out and waited on the side of the set while the studio audience were warmed up by the studio comic, quite often in the guise of Felix Bowness who portrayed the jockey Fred Quilley from *Hi De Hi*. At a given cue Felix stopped entertaining the audience and asked them to give a huge 'Allo 'Allo welcome to the café owner René Artois. To tumultuous applause, out walked Rene. He in turn introduced each and everyone of the gang with little quips like, 'Yvette nearly did not make it here tonight, no, she nearly had an accident; she swerved to avoid a child and fell off the bed! The audience would then cheer the roof off as Yvette came out to take a bow. Everybody had their own little joke from René as they were individually introduced to the studio audience including Mimi who ran out after René had said, 'Now here is someone who at her size has no problem keeping her ear to the ground, that pint-sized "Pocket Dynamo", the one, the only, Mimi Labonq!'

The episode then began in front of the live studio audience, with the cast hoping their comedy egg and chips would work and they would all be funny, because the writers would not allow any 'canned laughter'—an extra track of recorded laughter-- to be added to the show once that episode had finished.

The last episode finished with a scene filmed on location and later played to the audience. It was Madame Edith saying to René, 'René, what are you doing with that serving girl?' and René replying, 'You stupid woman! Can you not see I am eloping?' He then drives off from the town square with Yvette in his car and the rest of the gang chasing after him. The signature tune strikes up and the credits start to roll. The audience applaud and cheer tirelessly as the full cast now step off the set and stand in a full line up for the audience.

Then René stepped forward this special evening and addressed the audience: 'Ladies and gentlemen, I would just like to say, you are in actual fact witnessing a piece of history here tonight, because this is the very last time you will see this group of people standing together. On behalf of myself and the entire cast I would like to thank you all for the years of love and support you have given us -- now I would just ask the cast of *'Allo 'Allo* to say "Goodbye Goodbye" and take a final bow for the very last time.'

As you can imagine, there was not a dry eye in the house. With the blink of an eye it was all over.

'THE GANG'

THE 'ALLO 'ALLO CAN-CAN

Once upon a time ago a series called 'Allo 'Allo
Was written for the BBC by David Croft and Jeremy
It started back in '82 then 90 eps were made to view
Helga, Yvette, Mimi too, the three dynamic
bombshells

Madam Edith never really stood a chance
In the café she couldn't sing she couldn't dance
A partaker who was called Monsieur Alfonse
Said he was the one to undertake her

Listen very carefully I will say this only once
But if you don't I will repeat it once again
I'll give you an instance Michelle of the Resistance
Donned a mac and beret hence her
That she looked more like Frank Spencer

Lieutenant Gruber he was gay, I don't mean having
a nice day
He wanted René any way no matter what the time
of day

He'd have a snifter at the bar it never got him very
far
We'd all had René Artois
Except for Madame Edith

Colonel Von Strohm, Yvette drove him right off his head
In her bedroom I love you girl to death he said
Then he grabbed her and she fell right off the bed
She would say just to avoid a child, Hey!

Captain Albertorelli he liked Mimi very much
Till she kicked him in the crutch and said not on your nellie
Monsieur LeClerc the dandy, randy
Handled Madame Fanny and her flashing knobs

And don't forget Herr Flick and his sidekick von Smallhausen
The airman too von Klinkerhoffen who
Could forget that idiot Officer Crabtree
The biggest smash-hit on your BBC TV
Thank you David and Jeremy For every single repeat fee
Ha ha ha ..... Love .... Mimi! 'YOW'

© Sue Hodge 2003

ANOTHER COUNTRY

From the United Kingdom to the United States, from Sweden to Singapore, or Poland to Portugal, you name the country and they probably know or have heard of *'Allo 'Allo*. Around the world people have seen this program, more than Mimi has had hot dinners. In fact, the good people of Bulgaria have seen the series in its entirety twenty-two times as Mimi was told by the Bulgarian translator Zlatna Kostova. In France the series was dubbed into French, in Catalonia it was dubbed into Catalan and now something we all thought would never ever happen, it was going to be dubbed in-- German!

On the 10th of March 2008 a miracle took place; the national news headlines were, 'The Germans have bought *'Allo 'Allo.*'. The BBC announced that for the first time, the German channel ProSiebenSat.1 had bought the rights for the entire series. Until now Germany had perhaps understandably not picked up the series due to its subject matter, but it was now recognised that *'Allo 'Allo* was one of the most successful comedies ever made by the BBC and was much loved in over eighty countries. They pledged to do all they could to ensure that nothing was lost in translation, although this was going to be difficult for their script editors as there were so many jokes with double meanings in English.

It was down to the script's translating editor to find words in German meaning the same or nearly, and more often where one meaning is normal and the other naughty.

For example, Officer Crabtree's most famous catchphrase from the show 'Good Moaning,' in the German version becomes 'Guten Magen' which actually means 'Good stomach' in German and would not have had quite the same meaning as the English version. Mimi confessed she still would have fallen on the floor laughing if he had. Even so, one can see the translating problem. This of course was not the only problem, as Germans were not accustomed to seeing comedy shows about the war, so we wondered how this might be received? What would they really make of it? Would the German audience now actually find it funny? This remained to be seen. It might have taken them twenty-five years since the show was first aired in the U.K to buy the series (bearing in mind the war only took 6 years) but one thing was certain--both David Croft and Jeremy Lloyd were over the moon with what seemed to them a great coup.

A TALE OF TWO WITTIES

David Croft OBE (1922-2011)

David Croft was born on the 7th of September 1922 in Sandbanks, Poole, Dorset. He had an incredibly active life spanning 89 years, receiving The Writers Guild of Great Britain Award in 2003 for three consecutive years, The Lifetime Achievement Award at the British Comedy Awards, The Desmond Davies Award, and of course the OBE.

David was born into a showbiz family; his father, Reginald Sharland, enjoyed a successful career as a radio actor in Hollywood and his mother Annie Croft was a famous stage actress.

David enlisted in the Royal Artillery in 1942 and served during the Second World War. He also underwent officer training at the Royal Military College, Sandhurst, rising to the rank of Major. (Now, I wonder where the idea of Arthur Lowe as Captain Mainwaring came from?)

After his military service ended, David began work in the entertainment industry, writing many pantomimes. He worked for Tyne Tees Television before leaving to work for the BBC in the mid-1960s producing sitcoms such as *Beggar my Neighbour, Further Up Pompeii* and *Hugh and I.* It was while producing *Hugh and I* that he met an actor called Jimmy Perry, who handed him a script for a pilot program written about the British home guard during the Second World War. Liking this idea, David Croft and Jimmy Perry wrote nine series of a show called *Dad's Army* The rest is history ..... literally!

David Croft also went on to write *Are You Being Served?, It Ain't Half Hot Mum, Hi-De-Hi, You Rang, M'Lord?* and *Doctor Beeching*, and ta-da a world-wide smash hit with Jeremy Lloyd called *'Allo 'Allo*.

Mimi remembers a special conversation with this remarkable man; she told him how nervous she gets before going on stage. He responded, 'What, you? One of the greatest little stage performers ever? You're like a female Charlie Chaplin!'

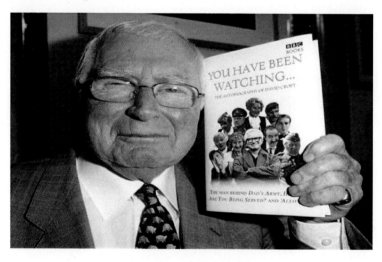

David Croft OBE

Jeremy Lloyd OBE (1930-2014)

Born in Danbury Essex, Jeremy Lloyd was raised in Manchester by his grandmother. He first worked as a junior assistant in the menswear department at Simpsons of Piccadilly (Ring any bells?). Jeremy Lloyd freely admitted that many of the characters depicted in the BBC television series *Are You Being Served?* came from this experience. He began his writing career in 1958 and also acted in numerous films and television comedies, becoming a regular on an American comedy sketch show called *Rowan & Martin's Laugh-In.*

The Americans loved his English upper-class twit depictions and he was highly praised and acclaimed. After returning to England he met and married the English actress and his second wife, Joanna Lumley; although the marriage didn't last, he never returned to the States.

He co-wrote with David Croft from 1972-1992 with *Are You Being Served* and *'Allo 'Allo* , He published his autobiography in 1993 entitled, *Listen Very Carefully, I Shall Say This Only Once.*

Jeremy Lloyd OBE

THE DIRECTOR'S NOTE

Although David Croft directed the pilot of *'Allo 'Allo* and thirty further episodes, other directors of great esteem brought their skill and talent to the series.

Martin Dennis was born in Toronto, Ontario, Canada and later lived in Surrey. He studied drama and Theatre Arts at Birmingham University before becoming a stage manager with the M6 Theatre Company. Martin then joined the BBC in 1980 as a floor manager, progressing to production manager on *Don't Wait Up*, *Hi De Hi* and *The Kenny Everett Show*, he then became a director on *'Allo 'Allo* In 1987 and adapted the show for a US market. He also adapted the American sitcom *Who's the Boss ?* for the UK, turning it into the highly successful *The Upper Hand* for Central TV , Martin directed three series.

He is also known for his direction on *Men Behaving Badly*, *Coupling My Good Friend*, and is currently directing *Carrie and Barrie* for Hartswood Films and BBC1. He was nominated for a BAFTA in the categories 'Comedy and Comedy Entertainment Programs' and awarded a BAFTA for 'Best Scripted Comedy'.

Robin Carr
Producer/Executive Producer directed thirty-three episodes of the comedy series *Second Thoughts*. He is known for *The Piglet Files, Smith and Jones, Time After Time, The Two of Us, Hi De Hi,* and *'Allo 'Allo.* He was also the guest star of *The Story of Are You Being Served?*

Richard Boden was born in Birmingham. He is a British television director and producer best known for *'Allo 'Allo, Blackadder Goes Forth, Life of Ri*ley and *The It Crowd.* He started his career at the BBC but was later Head of Comedy for Carlton and Central Television before going freelance.

Susan Belbin was born in Inverness, Scotland. She was a television director and producer whose work includes *'Allo 'Allo, One Foot in the Grave, Only Fools and Horses, Jonathon Creek,* and *Nelson's Column.* In 1992 she was awarded a BAFTA for 'Best Comedy' *(One Foot in the Grave), and in 1998, 'Best Drama Series'.* Jonathan Creek. In 1998 she retired due to ill health.

Mike Stephens is known for directing *Last of the Summer Wine* and *The Brittas Empire* and shared the 1990 season of directing *'Allo 'Allo* with Sue Longstaff. He is also noted for producing the BBC dramatization of David Walliam's novel *The Boy In The Dress*.

John B Hobbs arrived to direct the final two series of *'Allo 'Allo*. He was a well known favourite of the BBC, with an impressive track record for producing and directing shows such as *Bread*, *Three Up Two Down*, *Mulberry* and *Butterflies*.

Mimi: "The Complete Works"

Good Staff Are Hard To Find

(Series 4, Episode 3)

With Maria 'lost in the post', René and Edith are auditioning for a new serving girl - unsurprisingly, it seems that the two are looking for entirely different qualities! Meanwhile, with the Italians now in the war, Captain Alberto Bertorelli arrives at the château.

René interviews applicants for Maria's old job, but Michelle appoints Mimi, a fanatical Resistance colleague. Captain Bertorelli joins the Colonel's command as Liaison Officer for the Italians.

Dramatis Personae

Gorden Kaye	René François Artois
Carmen Silvera	Edith Melba Artois
Vicki Michelle	Yvette Carte-Blanche
Richard Marner	Colonel Kurt von Strohm
Kim Hartman	Private Helga Geerhart
Guy Siner	Lieutenant Hubert Gruber

Kirsten Cooke	Michelle Dubois
Richard Gibson	Herr Otto Flick
Rose Hill	Madame Fanny 'Fifi' Lafanne
Jack Haig	Monsieur Roger LeClerc
John D. Collins	Flt. Lt. Fairfax
Nicholas Frankau	Flt. Lt. Carstairs
Hilary Minster	General von Klinkerhoffen
Arthur Bostrom	Officer Crabtree
Gavin Richards	Captain Alberto Bertorelli
Sue Hodge	Mimi Labonq
Aimée Delamain	Madame Sablon
Estelle Matthews	Mademoiselle Vendome
Patrick Edwards	Guard

The Flying Nun

(Series 4, Episode 4)

With invasion plans afoot, and new waitress Mimi Labonq proving to be equal help and hindrance, Michelle supplies René with a newer, more powerful radio - as long as it can get a good signal.

The news is that the Germans are about to invade England. Flick, suspecting the Colonel and Von Klinkerhoffen of plotting to assassinate Hitler, infiltrates the Colonel's office to plant a bug.

Dramatis Personae

Gorden Kaye	René François Artois
Carmen Silvera	Edith Melba Artois
Vicki Michelle	Yvette Carte-Blanche
Sue Hodge	Mimi Labonq
Richard Marner	Colonel Kurt von Strohm
Gavin Richards	Captain Alberto Bertorelli
Kim Hartman	Private Helga Geerhart
Guy Siner	Lieutenant Hubert Gruber

Kirsten Cooke	Michelle Dubois
Richard Gibson	Herr Otto Flick
Rose Hill	Fanny 'Fifi' Lafanne
Jack Haig	Monsieur Roger LeClerc
John D. Collins	Flt. Lt. Fairfax
Nicholas Frankau	Flt. Lt. Carstairs
Hilary Minster	General von Klinkerhoffen
Kenneth Connor	Monsieur Alfonse
Arthur Bostrom	Officer Crabtree
John Louis Mansi	Engelbert von Smallhausen
Bill Malin	Soldier

The Sausages In The Trousers

(Series 4, Episode 5)

The Resistance begin sending through components to replace those lost from the radio (with the flying nun attached!) - Gruber, meanwhile, has finished the painting forgeries, and a shipment of dynamite has also arrived. The problem? They're all hidden inside sausages...

The secret radio is being powered by a tandem dynamo until stolen submarine batteries can arrive. The spy camera sent from London has fallen into a vineyard where the peasants are currently refusing to work for fear of being shot by the Communists.

Dramatis Personae

Gorden Kaye	René François Artois
Carmen Silvera	Edith Melba Artois
Vicki Michelle	Yvette Carte-Blanche
Sue Hodge	Mimi Labonq
Richard Marner	Colonel Kurt von Strohm
Gavin Richards	Captain Alberto Bertorelli

Kim Hartman	Private Helga Geerhart
Guy Siner	Lieutenant Hubert Gruber
Kirsten Cooke	Michelle Dubois
Richard Gibson	Herr Otto Flick
Rose Hill	Madame Fanny 'Fifi' Lafanne
Jack Haig	Monsieur Roger LeClerc
John D. Collins	Flt. Lt. Fairfax
Nicholas Frankau	Flt. Lt. Carstairs
Hilary Minster	General von Klinkerhoffen
Kenneth Connor	Monsieur Alfonse
Arthur Bostrom	Officer Crabtree
John Louis Mansi	Engelbert von Smallhausen
Trevor T. Smith	German Guard
Paul Cooper	London Calling' (Voice)
Bill Malin	Soldier
Stephen Churchett	Wing Commander Belfridge

The Jet Propelled Mother-In-Law

(Series 4, Episode 6)

René is arrested by the Colonel; in exchange for his release, he agrees to hide the original *Fallen Madonna* in his cellar. Just outside Nouvion, the General commandeers a set of vineyards and enlists everyone in the café to help pick the grapes.

Several of our cast come up with plans to attempt to rescue Herr Flick from the dungeon of von Klinkerhoffen. Meanwhile, Flick is on the rack and Edith succeeds in blowing up a portion of Nouvion.

Dramatis Personae

Gorden Kaye	René François Artois
Carmen Silvera	Edith Melba Artois
Vicki Michelle	Yvette Carte-Blanche
Sue Hodge	Mimi Labonq
Richard Marner	Colonel Kurt von Strohm
Gavin Richards	Captain Alberto Bertorelli
Kim Hartman	Private Helga Geerhart

Guy Siner	Lieutenant Hubert Gruber
Kirsten Cooke	Michelle Dubois
Richard Gibson	Herr Otto Flick
Rose Hill	Madame Fanny 'Fifi' Lafanne
Jack Haig	Monsieur Roger LeClerc
John D. Collins	Flt. Lt. Fairfax
Nicholas Frankau	Flt. Lt. Carstairs
Hilary Minster	General von Klinkerhoffen
Kenneth Connor	Monsieur Alfonse
Arthur Bostrom	Officer Crabtree
John Louis Mansi	Engelbert von Smallhausen
Trevor T. Smith	German Guard
James Gow	German Soldier
Howard Leader	Sergeant

Desperate Doings In The Dungeon

(Series 5, Episode 1)

Captain Bertorelli moves into Café René's spare room, and in on Madame Edith. Meanwhile, Michelle has Mimi and Yvette raid the Colonel's quarters for photographic film, and René...well, he has to help rescue Herr Flick...

There is a plan afoot to micro-photograph Hitler's invasion plans and to send them off to London. But first, Yvette and Mimi must distract the Colonel in order that they might obtain the necessary film.

Dramatis Personae

Gorden Kaye	René François Artois
Carmen Silvera	Edith Melba Artois
Vicki Michelle	Yvette Carte-Blanche
Sue Hodge	Mimi Labonq
Richard Marner	Colonel Kurt von Strohm
Gavin Richards	Captain Alberto Bertorelli
Kim Hartman	Private Helga Geerhart
Guy Siner	Lieutenant Hubert Gruber

Kirsten Cooke	Michelle Dubois
Richard Gibson	Herr Otto Flick
Rose Hill	Fanny 'Fifi' Lafanne
Jack Haig	Monsieur Roger LeClerc
John D. Collins	Flt. Lt. Fairfax
Nicholas Frankau	Flt. Lt. Carstairs
Hilary Minster	General von Klinkerhoffen
Kenneth Connor	Monsieur Alfonse
Arthur Bostrom	Officer Crabtree
John Louis Mansi	Engelbert von Smallhausen
Trevor T. Smith	German Guard
James Gow	German Soldier

The Camera In The Potato

(Series 5, Episode 2)

After Gruber rescues René from the dungeon, Michelle equips him with a camera disguised as a potato and sends the unwilling café owner straight back to the chateau in search of the safe containing the plans to invade England. Whose bedroom does fate dictate it's hidden in...?

Gruber rescues René from his cell. Flick orders Helga to collect evidence of a supposed plot to blow up Hitler. The plan to steal the Colonel's film is put into operation at the café.

Dramatis Personae

Gorden Kaye	René François Artois
Carmen Silvera	Edith Melba Artois
Vicki Michelle	Yvette Carte-Blanche
Sue Hodge	Mimi Labonq
Richard Marner	Colonel Kurt von Strohm
Kim Hartman	Private Helga Geerhart
Guy Siner	Lieutenant Hubert Gruber

Kirsten Cooke	Michelle Dubois
Richard Gibson	Herr Otto Flick
Rose Hill	Fanny 'Fifi' Lafanne
Jack Haig	Monsieur Roger LeClerc
John D. Collins	Flt. Lt. Fairfax
Nicholas Frankau	Flt. Lt. Carstairs
Hilary Minster	General von Klinkerhoffen
Kenneth Connor	Monsieur Alfonse
Arthur Bostrom	Officer Crabtree
Paul Cooper	London Calling' (Voice)
Martin Sadler	Gibson (Voice)
Patrick Edwards	Soldier in Café

Dinner With The General

(Series 5, Episode 3)

René is sent back to Gruber's bedroom, in the guise of a fireman and accompanied by LeClerc, tasked with blowing open the safe. Unfortunately for him, it seems that everyone else is at the chateau too...

Helga informs the Colonel and Gruber that Flick suspects they are plotting to kill Hitler. René and his staff develop a plan whereby LeClerc can enter Gruber's room disguised as a fireman to create a diversion so they can blow up the safe.

Dramatis Personae

Gorden Kaye	René François Artois
Carmen Silvera	Edith Melba Artois
Vicki Michelle	Yvette Carte-Blanche
Sue Hodge	Mimi Labonq
Richard Marner	Colonel Kurt von Strohm
Gavin Richards	Captain Alberto Bertorelli
Kim Hartman	Private Helga Geerhart

Guy Siner	Lieutenant Hubert Gruber
Kirsten Cooke	Michelle Dubois
Richard Gibson	Herr Otto Flick
Rose Hill	Fanny 'Fifi' Lafanne
Jack Haig	Monsieur Roger LeClerc
John D. Collins	Flt. Lt. Fairfax
Nicholas Frankau	Flt. Lt. Carstairs
Hilary Minster	General von Klinkerhoffen
Kenneth Connor	Monsieur Alfonse
Arthur Bostrom	Officer Crabtree
John Louis Mansi	Engelbert von Smallhausen
Patrick Edwards	German Guard

The Dreaded Circular Saw

(Series 5, Episode 4)

In the confusion of the chateau 'fire', René and LeClerc - now in full German uniform - are captured by the Communist Resistance and held captive in an old sawmill. Meanwhile, the Colonel is distraught to learn that the original *Fallen Madonna* and van Gogh have gone missing.

During the pandemonium caused by the fire at the chateau, LeClerc breaks into the safe and finds the *Fallen Madonna* and the van Gogh instead of the invasion plans. He nicks these and escapes disguised as a German.

Dramatis Personae

Gorden Kaye	René François Artois
Carmen Silvera	Edith Melba Artois
Vicki Michelle	Yvette Carte-Blanche
Sue Hodge	Mimi Labonq
Richard Marner	Colonel Kurt von Strohm
Gavin Richards	Captain Alberto Bertorelli

Kim Hartman	Private Helga Geerhart
Guy Siner	Lieutenant Hubert Gruber
Kirsten Cooke	Michelle Dubois
Richard Gibson	Herr Otto Flick
Rose Hill	Fanny 'Fifi' Lafanne
Jack Haig	Monsieur Roger LeClerc
John D. Collins	Flt. Lt. Fairfax
Nicholas Frankau	Flt. Lt. Carstairs
Hilary Minster	General von Klinkerhoffen
Kenneth Connor	Monsieur Alfonse
Arthur Bostrom	Officer Crabtree
John Louis Mansi	Engelbert von Smallhausen
Moira Foot	Denise Laroque Leader of the Communist Resistance
Carole Ashby	Louise (Communist Girl)

Otherwise Engaged

Series 5, Episode 5

When Denise recognises René as her long-lost childhood sweetheart, she sets him free -- after beginning arrangements for their wedding. Meanwhile, Helga continues working her way into Gruber's confidence.

René announces to Edith that he will marry the head of the Communist Resistance, Denise, who was his childhood sweetheart; no man has ever said 'No' to Denise before and lived to tell the tale.

Dramatis Personae

Gorden Kaye	René François Artois
Carmen Silvera	Edith Melba Artois
Vicki Michelle	Yvette Carte-Blanche
Sue Hodge	Mimi Labonq
Richard Marner	Colonel Kurt von Strohm
Gavin Richards	Captain Alberto Bertorelli
Kim Hartman	Private Helga Geerhart
Guy Siner	Lieutenant Hubert Gruber

Kirsten Cooke	Michelle Dubois
Richard Gibson	Herr Otto Flick
Rose Hill	Fanny 'Fifi' Lafanne
Jack Haig	Monsieur Roger LeClerc
John D. Collins	Flt. Lt. Fairfax
Nicholas Frankau	Flt. Lt. Carstairs
Hilary Minster	General von Klinkerhoffen
Kenneth Connor	Monsieur Alfonse
Arthur Bostrom	Officer Crabtree
John Louis Mansi	Engelbert von Smallhausen
Moira Foot	Denise Laroque Leader of the Communist Resistance
Carole Ashby	Louise (Communist Girl)

A Marriage Of Inconvenience

(Series 5, Episode 6)

As René's wedding approaches, Edith grows increasingly wistful for their past together. Unknown to René, she plots with Michelle -- for the good of the Resistance, naturally -- to take Denise's place at the altar.

René's wedding to Denise is on Saturday. Edith plots with Michelle to capture the bride and to stand in her place at the altar. Alphonse still hopes to marry Edith once René is out of the picture.

Dramatis Personae

Gorden Kaye	René François Artois
Carmen Silvera	Edith Melba Artois
Vicki Michelle	Yvette Carte-Blanche
Sue Hodge	Mimi Labonq
Richard Marner	Colonel Kurt von Strohm
Gavin Richards	Captain Alberto Bertorelli
Kim Hartman	Private Helga Geerhart
Guy Siner	Lieutenant Hubert Gruber

Kirsten Cooke	Michelle Dubois
Richard Gibson	Herr Otto Flick
Rose Hill	Fanny 'Fifi' Lafanne
Jack Haig	Monsieur Roger LeClerc
John D. Collins	Flt. Lt. Fairfax
Nicholas Frankau	Flt. Lt. Carstairs
Hilary Minster	General von Klinkerhoffen
Kenneth Connor	Monsieur Alfonse
Arthur Bostrom	Officer Crabtree
John Louis Mansi	Engelbert von Smallhausen
Moira Foot	Denise Laroque Leader of the Communist Resistance
Carole Ashby	Louise (Communist Girl)

No Hiding Place

(Series 5, Episode 7)

Upon hearing that Denise has escaped, René disguises himself as his own father and searches for a safe hiding place. With the café machine-gunned, Denise's followers capture René - but it is not René she is out to get.

In the aftermath of her wedding day, Denise has escaped and is out for blood. The café is machine gunned. René wisely takes on the disguise of his father and seeks sanctuary from the Colonel.

Dramatis Personae

Gorden Kaye	René François Artois
Carmen Silvera	Edith Melba Artois
Vicki Michelle	Yvette Carte-Blanche
Sue Hodge	Mimi Labonq
Richard Marner	Colonel Kurt von Strohm
Kim Hartman	Private Helga Geerhart
Guy Siner	Lieutenant Hubert Gruber
Kirsten Cooke	Michelle Dubois

Richard Gibson	Herr Otto Flick
Rose Hill	Fanny 'Fifi' Lafanne
Jack Haig	Monsieur Roger LeClerc
John D. Collins	Flt. Lt. Fairfax
Nicholas Frankau	Flt. Lt. Carstairs
Hilary Minster	General von Klinkerhoffen
Kenneth Connor	Monsieur Alfonse
Arthur Bostrom	Officer Crabtree
John Louis Mansi	Engelbert von Smallhausen
Moira Foot	Denise Laroque Leader of the Communist Resistance
Carole Ashby	Louise (Communist Girl)
Phoebe Scholfield	Communist Resistance Girl
John Rutland	Deliveryman
Christopher Gray	German Soldier
Richard Bonehill	German Guard

The Arrival Of The Homing Duck

(Series 5, Episode 8)

With the General breathing ever-closer down his neck over the location of the paintings, the Colonel issues René an ultimatum. Meanwhile, Michelle explains her plans for a long-distance duck to transport the microfilm, and Madame Edith goes into hiding, disguised as LeClerc.

René tells Edith, Yvette and Mimi that Denise is out to get them. Edith is frightened into disguising herself first as her mother and then as LeClerc. Helga reports the whereabouts of the paintings to the Colonel.

Dramatis Personae

Gorden Kaye	René François Artois
Carmen Silvera	Edith Melba Artois
Vicki Michelle	Yvette Carte-Blanche
Sue Hodge	Mimi Labonq
Richard Marner	Colonel Kurt von Strohm
Gavin Richards	Captain Alberto Bertorelli

Kim Hartman	Private Helga Geerhart
Guy Siner	Lieutenant Hubert Gruber
Kirsten Cooke	Michelle Dubois
Richard Gibson	Herr Otto Flick
Rose Hill	Fanny 'Fifi' Lafanne
Jack Haig	Monsieur Roger LeClerc
John D. Collins	Flt. Lt. Fairfax
Nicholas Frankau	Flt. Lt. Carstairs
Hilary Minster	General von Klinkerhoffen
Kenneth Connor	Monsieur Alfonse
Arthur Bostrom	Officer Crabtree
John Louis Mansi	Engelbert von Smallhausen
Patrick Edwards	German Guard
John Readman	Italian Soldier

Watch The Birdie

(Series 5, Episode 9)

It is, finally, time for the Generals' Conference and the planning of the invasion of England. The Resistance furnish René with another suitably ridiculous photographic device to capture their plans. But it could all go awry if Mimi kills one of the attendees before the day...

Michelle gives René an outfit in which he can conceal the camera so he can take pictures of the invasion plans. Café René is doing the catering for the Meeting of the Generals, so the stage is set for photographic intrigue.

Dramatis Personae

Gorden Kaye	René François Artois
Carmen Silvera	Edith Melba Artois
Vicki Michelle	Yvette Carte-Blanche
Sue Hodge	Mimi Labonq
Richard Marner	Colonel Kurt von Strohm
Gavin Richards	Captain Alberto Bertorelli

Kim Hartman	Private Helga Geerhart
Guy Siner	Lieutenant Hubert Gruber
Kirsten Cooke	Michelle Dubois
Richard Gibson	Herr Otto Flick
Rose Hill	Fanny 'Fifi' Lafanne
Jack Haig	Monsieur Roger LeClerc
John D. Collins	Flt. Lt. Fairfax
Nicholas Frankau	Flt. Lt. Carstairs
Hilary Minster	General von Klinkerhoffen
Kenneth Connor	Monsieur Alfonse
Arthur Bostrom	Officer Crabtree
John Louis Mansi	Engelbert von Smallhausen
Paul Cooper	London Calling' (Voice)
Tim Brown	Tailor
Ken Morley	General von Flockenstuffen

René - Under An Assumed Nose

(Series 5, Episode 10)

Once again, René goes into hiding when it is believed that he was behind a plot to kill the Generals at their invasion meeting. Unfortunately, he chooses to disguise himself as a General...

The previous week's photographic efforts were, after all, unsuccessful. Seems there were not any actual invasion plans on the map which René photographed. Michelle reveals her love for René.

Dramatis Personae

Gorden Kaye	René François Artois
Carmen Silvera	Edith Melba Artois
Vicki Michelle	Yvette Carte-Blanche
Sue Hodge	Mimi Labonq
Richard Marner	Colonel Kurt von Strohm
Gavin Richards	Captain Alberto Bertorelli
Kim Hartman	Private Helga Geerhart
Guy Siner	Lieutenant Hubert Gruber

Kirsten Cooke	Michelle Dubois
Richard Gibson	Herr Otto Flick
Rose Hill	Fanny 'Fifi' Lafanne
Jack Haig	Monsieur Roger LeClerc
John D. Collins	Flt. Lt. Fairfax
Nicholas Frankau	Flt. Lt. Carstairs
Hilary Minster	General von Klinkerhoffen
Kenneth Connor	Monsieur Alfonse
Arthur Bostrom	Officer Crabtree
John Louis Mansi	Engelbert von Smallhausen
Paul Cooper	'London Calling' (Voice)
Richard Bonehill	German Guard
Dick Harris	Storm-trooper

The Confusion Of The Generals

(Series 5, Episode 11)

With a French General now under suspicion for attempting to poison the Germans, René's café is suddenly overrun with French peasants - and if that weren't bad enough, the RAF are paying a visit...

Gruber informs Von Klinkerhoffen that it was the collaborating French General who blew up Flick and is suspected of trying to poison the other Generals. René is reprieved. Michelle tells Yvette she is faking her love for René so he will remain in the Resistance.

Dramatis Personae

Gorden Kaye	René François Artois
Carmen Silvera	Edith Melba Artois
Vicki Michelle	Yvette Carte-Blanche
Sue Hodge	Mimi Labonq
Richard Marner	Colonel Kurt von Strohm
Kim Hartman	Private Helga Geerhart

Guy Siner	Lieutenant Hubert Gruber
Kirsten Cooke	Michelle Dubois
Richard Gibson	Herr Otto Flick
Rose Hill	Fanny 'Fifi' Lafanne
Jack Haig	Monsieur Roger LeClerc
John D. Collins	Flt. Lt. Fairfax
Nicholas Frankau	Flt. Lt. Carstairs
Hilary Minster	General von Klinkerhoffen
Kenneth Connor	Monsieur Alfonse
Arthur Bostrom	Officer Crabtree
John Louis Mansi	Engelbert von Smallhausen
Patrick Edwards	German Guard
Ken Morley	General von Flockenstuffen
Fred Bryant	German General

Who's For The Vatican?

(Series 5, Episode 12)

All hell is breaking loose in Nouvion: the captured Generals are free, von Klinkerhoffen is sending Gruber and Colonel von Strohm to the Russian front, and René is sent to collect the paintings before helping them escape to South America!

Fearing being blamed for the ten Generals who were sent to the coast, René sets out to brick himself into his cellar. Michelle arrives with a medal for his bravery but also with a suicide pill since he knows too much.

Dramatis Personae

Gorden Kaye	René François Artois
Carmen Silvera	Edith Melba Artois
Vicki Michelle	Yvette Carte-Blanche
Sue Hodge	Mimi Labonq
Richard Marner	Colonel Kurt von Strohm
Kim Hartman	Private Helga Geerhart
Guy Siner	Lieutenant Hubert Gruber

Kirsten Cooke	Michelle Dubois
Richard Gibson	Herr Otto Flick
Rose Hill	Fanny 'Fifi' Lafanne
Jack Haig	Monsieur Roger LeClerc
John D. Collins	Flt. Lt. Fairfax
Nicholas Frankau	Flt. Lt. Carstairs
Hilary Minster	General von Klinkerhoffen
Kenneth Connor	Monsieur Alfonse
Arthur Bostrom	Officer Crabtree
John Louis Mansi	Engelbert von Smallhausen
Moira Foot	Denise Laroque Leader of the Communist Resistance
Carole Ashby	Louise (Communist Girl)
Trevor T. Smith	German Guard
John Readman	Italian Soldier
Jacqueline Ashman	Michelle's Assistant

Ribbing The Bonk

(Series 5, Episode 13)

Mimi, Gruber, Bertorelli and the Colonel are held at the Communist Resistance's secret headquarters. René escapes with message of their ransom: one million francs. General von Klinkerhoffen, however, is not keen to pay.

The Colonel, Gruber, Bertorelli and LeClerc are held to ransom by Denise and the Communists. Michelle learns of the situation and decides this is an opportune time to do away with both the Germans and the Communists.

Dramatis Personae

Gorden Kaye	René François Artois
Carmen Silvera	Edith Melba Artois
Vicki Michelle	Yvette Carte-Blanche
Sue Hodge	Mimi Labonq
Richard Marner	Colonel Kurt von Strohm
Gavin Richards	Captain Alberto Bertorelli
Kim Hartman	Private Helga Geerhart

Guy Siner	Lieutenant Hubert Gruber
Kirsten Cooke	Michelle Dubois
Richard Gibson	Herr Otto Flick
Rose Hill	Madame Fanny 'Fifi' Lafanne
Jack Haig	Monsieur Roger LeClerc
John D. Collins	Flt. Lt. Fairfax
Nicholas Frankau	Flt. Lt. Carstairs
Hilary Minster	General von Klinkerhoffen
Kenneth Connor	Monsieur Alfonse
Arthur Bostrom	Officer Crabtree
John Louis Mansi	Engelbert von Smallhausen
Moira Foot	Denise Laroque Leader of the Communist Resistance
Carole Ashby	Louise (Communist Girl)
Jackie D. Broad	Communist Girl
Eddie Caswell	Fruit Seller
Owen Brenman	'London Calling' (Voice)

The Reluctant Millionaires

Series 5, Episode 14

When Mimi appears in the square with news that the General freed everyone from the Communists, René and co. are delighted that they will not need to pay the ransom. But upon learning who the stolen money actually belongs to, they are soon desperately trying to get rid...

The stolen money from the bank robbery is hidden in the cuckoo clock. Concerned because Edith's singing is driving away the paying customers, René tries to convince her instead to mime to a Jeanette McDonald record.

Dramatis Personae

Gorden Kaye	René François Artois
Carmen Silvera	Edith Melba Artois
Vicki Michelle	Yvette Carte-Blanche
Sue Hodge	Mimi Labonq
Richard Marner	Colonel Kurt Von Strohm
Gavin Richards	Captain Alberto Bertorelli

Kim Hartman	Private Helga Geerhart
Guy Siner	Lieutenant Hubert Gruber
Kirsten Cooke	Michelle Dubois
Richard Gibson	Herr Otto Flick
Rose Hill	Fanny 'Fifi' Lafanne
Jack Haig	Monsieur Roger LeClerc
John D. Collins	Flt. Lt. Fairfax
Nicholas Frankau	Flt. Lt. Carstairs
Hilary Minster	General von Klinkerhoffen
Kenneth Connor	Monsieur Alfonse
Arthur Bostrom	Officer Crabtree
John Louis Mansi	Engelbert von Smallhausen
Moira Foot	Denise Laroque Leader of the Communist Resistance
Carole Ashby	Louise (Communist Girl)

A Duck For Launch

(Series 5, Episode 15)

Whilst Denise Laroque hides in his cellar, Michelle orders René to dispatch the long-distance duck to England, with microfilm attached. Meanwhile, Flick and von Smallhausen are on the hunt for the missing money.

Flick and von Smallhausen disguise themselves as fish traders to trace his stolen money. Michelle arrives at the café with the microfilm of the invasion plans to attach to the long-distance duck which must leave today.

Dramatis Personae

Gorden Kaye	René François Artois
Carmen Silvera	Edith Melba Artois
Vicki Michelle	Yvette Carte-Blanche
Sue Hodge	Mimi Labonq
Richard Marner	Colonel Kurt von Strohm
Gavin Richards	Captain Alberto Bertorelli
Kim Hartman	Private Helga Geerhart

Guy Siner	Lieutenant Hubert Gruber
Kirsten Cooke	Michelle Dubois
Richard Gibson	Herr Otto Flick
Rose Hill	Fanny 'Fifi' Lafanne
Jack Haig	Monsieur Roger LeClerc
John D. Collins	Flt. Lt. Fairfax
Nicholas Frankau	Flt. Lt. Carstairs
Hilary Minster	General von Klinkerhoffen
Kenneth Connor	Monsieur Alfonse
Arthur Bostrom	Officer Crabtree
John Louis Mansi	Engelbert von Smallhausen
Moira Foot	Denise Laroque Leader of the Communist Resistance
Carole Ashby	Louise (Communist Girl)
Christopher Gray	German Soldier
Owen Brenman	Kingfisher (Voice)

The Exploding Bedpan

(Series 5, Episode 16)

Monsieur Alfonse suffers a heart attack in Flick's lair, whilst under interrogation regarding the stolen money. Naturally, Michelle has a plan to liberate him before he spills the beans.

Despite the unsuccessful attempt to launch the long-distance duck, René hopes life can return to normal. But he hasn't reckoned with the passions of Yvette, Mimi, Denise, and now, Louise.

Dramatis Personae

Gorden Kaye	René François Artois
Carmen Silvera	Edith Melba Artois
Vicki Michelle	Yvette Carte-Blanche
Sue Hodge	Mimi Labonq
Richard Marner	Colonel Kurt von Strohm
Gavin Richards	Captain Alberto Bertorelli
Kim Hartman	Private Helga Geerhart
Guy Siner	Lieutenant Hubert Gruber

Kirsten Cooke	Michelle Dubois
Richard Gibson	Herr Otto Flick
Rose Hill	Fanny 'Fifi' Lafanne
Jack Haig	Monsieur Roger LeClerc
John D. Collins	Flt. Lt. Fairfax
Nicholas Frankau	Flt. Lt. Carstairs
Hilary Minster	General von Klinkerhoffen
Kenneth Connor	Monsieur Alfonse
Arthur Bostrom	Officer Crabtree
John Louis Mansi	Engelbert von Smallhausen
Moira Foot	Denise Laroque Leader of the Communist Resistance
Carole Ashby	Louise (Communist Girl)
Lucinda Smith	Nurse
Stephen Reynolds	Surgeon
Owen Brenman	'French' London Operator
Julie-Christian Young	Cockney Mac Fisheries Girl

Going Like A Bomb

Series 5, Episode 17

With Monsieur Alfonse now considered by Herr Flick to have been exploded by a bedpan, the Colonel sets up Captain Bertorelli to be caught with the stolen - and forged - money. Unfortunately, nothing runs smoothly...

René returns from the hospital to learn from Gruber that Alfonse has been eliminated by an exploding bed pan. Michelle has concocted a new plan to drop Carstairs and Fairfax back into England.

Dramatis Personae

Gorden Kaye	René François Artois
Carmen Silvera	Edith Melba Artois
Vicki Michelle	Yvette Carte-Blanche
Sue Hodge	Mimi Labonq
Richard Marner	Colonel Kurt von Strohm
Gavin Richards	Captain Alberto Bertorelli
Kim Hartman	Private Helga Geerhart

Guy Siner	Lieutenant Hubert Gruber
Kirsten Cooke	Michelle Dubois
Richard Gibson	Herr Otto Flick
Rose Hill	Fanny 'Fifi' Lafanne
Jack Haig	Monsieur Roger LeClerc
John D. Collins	Flt. Lt. Fairfax
Nicholas Frankau	Flt. Lt. Carstairs
Hilary Minster	General von Klinkerhoffen
Kenneth Connor	Monsieur Alfonse
Arthur Bostrom	Officer Crabtree
John Louis Mansi	Engelbert von Smallhausen
Moira Foot	Denise Laroque Leader of the Communist Resistance
Carole Ashby	Louise (Communist Girl)

Money To Burn

Series 5, Episode 18

Time is running out for Monsieur LeClerc; if he does not reveal the whereabouts of the missing money, Flick will have him shot. If he DOES reveal the whereabouts of the missing money, Michelle will have him shot: will the RAF arrive in time?

Helga informs the Colonel that LeClerc will be shot if the stolen money is not returned. The Colonel sends Gruber to tell René to give back the money which is hidden in the café's oven. Meanwhile, Fanny decides to bake a potato.

Dramatis Personae

Gorden Kaye	René François Artois
Carmen Silvera	Edith Melba Artois
Vicki Michelle	Yvette Carte-Blanche
Sue Hodge	Mimi Labonq
Richard Marner	Colonel Kurt von Strohm
Gavin Richards	Captain Alberto Bertorelli
Kim Hartman	Private Helga Geerhart

Guy Siner	Lieutenant Hubert Gruber
Kirsten Cooke	Michelle Dubois
Richard Gibson	Herr Otto Flick
Rose Hill	Madame Fanny 'Fifi' Lafanne
Jack Haig	Monsieur Roger LeClerc
John D. Collins	Flt. Lt. Fairfax
Nicholas Frankau	Flt. Lt. Carstairs
Hilary Minster	General von Klinkerhoffen
Kenneth Connor	Monsieur Alfonse
Arthur Bostrom	Officer Crabtree
John Louis Mansi	Engelbert von Smallhausen
John Readman	Italian Soldier
Jacqueline Ashman	Michelle's Assistant

Puddings Can Go Off

(Series 5, Episode 19)

Michelle orders René to store 1,000 kg. of high explosives in his café - disguised as Christmas puddings! Herr Flick, meanwhile, is dealing with land mines.

Michelle tells René he must hide the explosives in the café. The materials will be brought in by Alfonse, Crabtree and 'pregnant' Resistance girls. The charges will be disguised as Christmas puddings.

Dramatis Personae

Gorden Kaye	René François Artois
Carmen Silvera	Edith Melba Artois
Vicki Michelle	Yvette Carte-Blanche
Sue Hodge	Mimi Labonq
Richard Marner	Colonel Kurt von Strohm
Gavin Richards	Captain Alberto Bertorelli
Kim Hartman	Private Helga Geerhart
Guy Siner	Lieutenant Hubert Gruber

Kirsten Cooke	Michelle Dubois
Richard Gibson	Herr Otto Flick
Rose Hill	Madame Fanny 'Fifi' Lafanne
Jack Haig	Monsieur Roger LeClerc
John D. Collins	Flt. Lt. Fairfax
Nicholas Frankau	Flt. Lt. Carstairs
Hilary Minster	General von Klinkerhoffen
Kenneth Connor	Monsieur Alfonse
Arthur Bostrom	Officer Crabtree
John Louis Mansi	Engelbert von Smallhausen
Phoebe Scholfield	Henriette Michelle's Assistant

Land Mines For London

(Series 5, Episode 20)

Plans to drop the British airmen over England and concealed inside land mines are progressing - but with Herr Flick's intervention, not going all that well. But things could be far worse at Café René if Yvette is not careful with her candles!

Helga has been spying on von Smallhausen and knows the land mines are in the builder's yard. When these are removed to the air base, Michelle tells René that the airmen will be smuggled in barrels disguised as beer for the Sergeant's mess.

Dramatis Personae

Gorden Kaye	René François Artois
Carmen Silvera	Edith Melba Artois
Vicki Michelle	Yvette Carte-Blanche
Sue Hodge	Mimi Labonq
Richard Marner	Colonel Kurt von Strohm
Gavin Richards	Captain Alberto Bertorelli
Kim Hartman	Private Helga Geerhart

Guy Siner	Lieutenant Hubert Gruber
Kirsten Cooke	Michelle Dubois
Richard Gibson	Herr Otto Flick
Rose Hill	Madame Fanny 'Fifi' Lafanne
Jack Haig	Monsieur Roger LeClerc
John D. Collins	Flt. Lt. Fairfax
Nicholas Frankau	Flt. Lt. Carstairs
Hilary Minster	General von Klinkerhoffen
Kenneth Connor	Monsieur Alfonse
Arthur Bostrom	Officer Crabtree
John Louis Mansi	Engelbert von Smallhausen
John Readman	Italian Soldier
Sion Tudor Owen	German Pilot
Steven Bronowski	German Navigator
James Charles	German Corporal
Chris Andrews	German Soldier

Flight To Geneva

(Series 5, Episode 21)

Michelle's latest scheme for the escape of the airmen (involving a mini-submarine) pushes René over the edge, and he attempts to elope with Yvette (and the two original paintings) to Switzerland.

But Flick finds out that Hitler does not want the paintings for himself. It's a trick by von Klinkerhoffen to get them for himself.

Dramatis Personae

Gorden Kaye	René François Artois
Carmen Silvera	Edith Melba Artois
Vicki Michelle	Yvette Carte-Blanche
Sue Hodge	Mimi Labonq
Richard Marner	Colonel Kurt von Strohm
Gavin Richards	Captain Alberto Bertorelli
Kim Hartman	Private Helga Geerhart
Guy Siner	Lieutenant Hubert Gruber

Kirsten Cooke	Michelle Dubois
Richard Gibson	Herr Otto Flick
Rose Hill	Madame Fanny 'Fifi' Lafanne
Jack Haig	Monsieur Roger LeClerc
John D. Collins	Flt. Lt. Fairfax
Nicholas Frankau	Flt. Lt. Carstairs
Hilary Minster	General von Klinkerhoffen
Kenneth Connor	Monsieur Alfonse
Arthur Bostrom	Officer Crabtree
John Louis Mansi	Engelbert von Smallhausen
Michael Percival	Yoop Hoop de Hoop (Swedish Art Expert)
Howard Leader	Train Ticket Seller
Neil West	Train Guard
John Leeson	Train's Waiter

Train Of Events

(Series 5, Episode 22)

The Colonel, Gruber and Helga are after the paintings, as are Flick and von Smallhausen. Mimi, Yvette and Madame Edith are after René. And they're all aboard the Geneva Express, which the Resistance is about to blow up with Christmas puddings...

René is on the night train to Geneva, and while he is seeking to avoid Edith, he bumps into Mimi, the Colonel and Gruber. René eventually finds Yvette, but the train is then blown up by exploding Christmas puddings.

Dramatis Personae

Gorden Kaye	René François Artois
Carmen Silvera	Edith Melba Artois
Vicki Michelle	Yvette Carte-Blanche
Sue Hodge	Mimi Labonq
Richard Marner	Colonel Kurt von Strohm
Gavin Richards	Captain Alberto Bertorelli

Kim Hartman	Private Helga Geerhart
Guy Siner	Lieutenant Hubert Gruber
Kirsten Cooke	Michelle Dubois
Richard Gibson	Herr Otto Flick
Rose Hill	Madame Fanny 'Fifi' Lafanne
Jack Haig	Monsieur Roger LeClerc
John D. Collins	Flt. Lt. Fairfax
Nicholas Frankau	Flt. Lt. Carstairs
Hilary Minster	General von Klinkerhoffen
Kenneth Connor	Monsieur Alfonse
Arthur Bostrom	Officer Crabtree
John Louis Mansi	Engelbert von Smallhausen
John Readman	Italian Soldier
Patrick Edwards	German Soldier

An Enigma Variation

(Series 5, Episode 23)

When the paintings are hidden inside a hollowed-out statue that is then requisitioned by the General, it falls on René and Co. to infiltrate one of Klinkerhoffen's parties and snatch them back.

René hides his gold in the cuckoo clock, then at the Colonel's order disguises himself and his Resistance friends as a string quartet to play at the Officer's dance. Flick and von Smallhausen attend the same dance disguised as maids.

Dramatis Personae

Gorden Kaye	René François Artois
Carmen Silvera	Edith Melba Artois
Vicki Michelle	Yvette Carte-Blanche
Sue Hodge	Mimi Labonq
Richard Marner	Colonel Kurt von Strohm
Gavin Richards	Captain Alberto Bertorelli
Kim Hartman	Private Helga Geerhart
Guy Siner	Lieutenant Hubert Gruber

Kirsten Cooke	Michelle Dubois
Richard Gibson	Herr Otto Flick
Rose Hill	Madame Fanny 'Fifi' Lafanne
Jack Haig	Monsieur Roger LeClerc
John D. Collins	Flt. Lt. Fairfax
Nicholas Frankau	Flt. Lt. Carstairs
Hilary Minster	General von Klinkerhoffen
Kenneth Connor	Monsieur Alfonse
Arthur Bostrom	Officer Crabtree
John Louis Mansi	Engelbert von Smallhausen
Paul Cooper	'London Calling' (Voice)
Ken Morley	General von Flockenstuffen
Fred Bryant	German General

Wedding Bliss

(Series 5, Episode 24)

Faced with the prospect of her marrying Monsieur Alfonse, René finally proposes and arranges his re-marriage to Edith. At the chateau, General von Klinkerhoffen is on the search for missing gold; Herr Flick is convinced that René knows its whereabouts.

René hides the missing paintings in packets of spaghetti. Edith tells René that she is marrying Monsieur Alfonse. Meanwhile, mine detector in hand, Von Klinkerhoffen scans the Colonel's office. He finds no gold, but he does find the Colonel's toupée.

Dramatis Personae

Gorden Kaye	René François Artois
Carmen Silvera	Edith Melba Artois
Vicki Michelle	Yvette Carte-Blanche
Sue Hodge	Mimi Labonq
Richard Marner	Colonel Kurt von Strohm
Gavin Richards	Captain Alberto Bertorelli

Kim Hartman	Private Helga Geerhart
Guy Siner	Lieutenant Hubert Gruber
Kirsten Cooke	Michelle Dubois
Richard Gibson	Herr Otto Flick
Rose Hill	Madame Fanny 'Fifi' Lafanne
Jack Haig	Monsieur Roger LeClerc
John D. Collins	Flt. Lt. Fairfax
Nicholas Frankau	Flt. Lt. Carstairs
Hilary Minster	General von Klinkerhoffen
Kenneth Connor	Monsieur Alfonse
Arthur Bostrom	Officer Crabtree
John Louis Mansi	Engelbert von Smallhausen
Howard Leader	German Guard

Down The Drain

(Series 5, Episode 25)

René is packing, once again, to elope with Yvette and the nicked gold to Switzerland - but before he goes, there's the small matter of a missing Enigma machine to deal with.

Yvette and Edith both question René about the whereabouts of the gold, but he is not talking. The Colonel and Gruber search Café René for the missing Enigma machine, but all they turn up is Yvette's new underwear.

Dramatis Personae

Gorden Kaye	René François Artois
Carmen Silvera	Edith Melba Artois
Vicki Michelle	Yvette Carte-Blanche
Sue Hodge	Mimi Labonq
Richard Marner	Colonel Kurt von Strohm
Guy Siner	Lieutenant Hubert Gruber
Kirsten Cooke	Michelle Dubois

Rose Hill	Madame Fanny 'Fifi' Lafanne
Jack Haig	Monsieur Roger LeClerc
John D. Collins	Flt. Lt. Fairfax
Nicholas Frankau	Flt. Lt. Carstairs
Hilary Minster	General von Klinkerhoffen
Kenneth Connor	Monsieur Alfonse
Arthur Bostrom	Officer Crabtree
David Lloyd	German Soldier

All In Disgeese

(Series 5, Episode 26)

Having failed to send the Enigma machine to Britain, two British Intelligence agents are on their way to Nouvion to examine the machine - a relief to René, who is just hours before being shot if it is not returned to the General!

Michelle calls an emergency meeting. She tells René and the others that two British experts are coming disguised as policemen to examine the Enigma machine. The Colonel is ordered to arrest and execute six most prominent town members if the machine is not returned.

Dramatis Personae

Gorden Kaye	René François Artois
Carmen Silvera	Edith Melba Artois
Vicki Michelle	Yvette Carte-Blanche
Sue Hodge	Mimi Labonq
Richard Marner	Colonel Kurt von Strohm
Gavin Richards	Captain Alberto Bertorelli

Kim Hartman	Private Helga Geerhart
Guy Siner	Lieutenant Hubert Gruber
Kirsten Cooke	Michelle Dubois
Richard Gibson	Herr Otto Flick
Rose Hill	Madame Fanny 'Fifi' Lafanne
Jack Haig	Monsieur Roger LeClerc
John D. Collins	Flt. Lt. Fairfax
Nicholas Frankau	Flt. Lt. Carstairs
Hilary Minster	General von Klinkerhoffen
Kenneth Connor	Monsieur Alfonse
Arthur Bostrom	Officer Crabtree
John Louis Mansi	Engelbert von Smallhausen
Philip Fox	British Agent
James Gow	British Agent 69
Robbin John	German Guard

Desperate Doings In The Graveyard (Series 6, Episode 1)

For a number of days and nights, a group of undertakers have been excavating in the graveyard, below René's empty tomb, in order to create a resistance communications centre. The flurry of activity has not failed to catch the General's eye!

Dramatis Personae

Gorden Kaye	René François Artois
Carmen Silvera	Edith Melba Artois
Vicki Michelle	Yvette Carte-Blanche
Sue Hodge	Mimi Labonq
Richard Marner	Colonel Kurt von Strohm
Gavin Richards	Captain Alberto Bertorelli
Kim Hartman	Private Helga Geerhart
Guy Siner	Lieutenant Hubert Gruber
Kirsten Cooke	Michelle Dubois

Richard Gibson	Herr Otto Flick
Rose Hill	Madame Fanny 'Fifi' Lafanne
John D. Collins	Flt. Lt. Fairfax
Nicholas Frankau	Flt. Lt. Carstairs
Hilary Minster	General von Klinkerhoffen
Kenneth Connor	Monsieur Alfonse
Arthur Bostrom	Officer Crabtree
John Louis Mansi	Engelbert von Smallhausen
Derek Royle	Monsieur Ernest LeClerc
Rikki Howard	Elaine

The Gestapo For The High Jump

(Series 6, Episode 2)

Herr Flick and Von Smallhausen are planning to disguise themselves as British airmen in order to be 'rescued' by the Resistance; when both the German Army and René discover this, it's certain that the plan won't come off...

Dramatis Personae

Gorden Kaye	René François Artois
Carmen Silvera	Edith Melba Artois
Vicki Michelle	Yvette Carte-Blanche
Sue Hodge	Mimi Labonq
Richard Marner	Colonel Kurt von Strohm
Gavin Richards	Captain Alberto Bertorelli
Kim Hartman	Private Helga Geerhart
Guy Siner	Lieutenant Hubert Gruber
Kirsten Cooke	Michelle Dubois
Richard Gibson	Herr Otto Flick

Rose Hill	Madame Fanny 'Fifi' Lafanne
John D. Collins	Flt. Lt. Fairfax
Nicholas Frankau	Flt. Lt. Carstairs
Hilary Minster	General von Klinkerhoffen
Kenneth Connor	Monsieur Alfonse
Arthur Bostrom	Officer Crabtree
John Louis Mansi	Engelbert von Smallhausen
Derek Royle	Monsieur Ernest LeClerc
Phoebe Scholfield	Henriette Michelle's Assistant
John Readman	Italian Soldier
Rikki Howard	Elaine

The Nouvion Oars

(Series 6, Episode 3)

As the airmen continue to attempt their escape under an upturned bathtub, the river estuary suddenly becomes incredibly crowded.

Dramatis Personae

Gorden Kaye	René François Artois
Carmen Silvera	Edith Melba Artois
Vicki Michelle	Yvette Carte-Blanche
Sue Hodge	Mimi Labonq
Richard Marner	Colonel Kurt von Strohm
Gavin Richards	Captain Alberto Bertorelli
Kim Hartman	Private Helga Geerhart
Guy Siner	Lieutenant Hubert Gruber
Kirsten Cooke	Michelle Dubois
Richard Gibson	Herr Otto Flick

Rose Hill	Madame Fanny 'Fifi' Lafanne
John D. Collins	Flt. Lt. Fairfax
Nicholas Frankau	Flt. Lt. Carstairs
Hilary Minster	General Von Klinkerhoffen
Kenneth Connor	Monsieur Alfonse
Arthur Bostrom	Officer Crabtree
John Louis Mansi	Engelbert on Smallhausen
Derek Royle	Monsieur Ernest LeClerc
Richard Seymour	German Guard
David Griffin	Submarine Commander
Tim Brown	Submarine Lieutenant

The Nicked Airmen

(Series 6, Episode 4)

The British Airmen have been arrested, and Michelle fears that they could reveal Nighthawk's identity under interrogation, so orders a daring rescue plan to take place in the dead of night.

Dramatis Personae

Gorden Kaye	René François Artois
Carmen Silvera	Edith Melba Artois
Vicki Michelle	Yvette Carte-Blanche
Sue Hodge	Mimi Labonq
Richard Marner	Colonel Kurt von Strohm
Gavin Richards	Captain Alberto Bertorelli
Kim Hartman	Private Helga Geerhart
Guy Siner	Lieutenant Hubert Gruber
Kirsten Cooke	Michelle Dubois
Richard Gibson	Herr Otto Flick

Rose Hill	Madame Fanny 'Fifi' Lafanne
John D. Collins	Flt. Lt. Fairfax
Nicholas Frankau	Flt. Lt. Carstairs
Hilary Minster	General von Klinkerhoffen
Kenneth Connor	Monsieur Alfonse
Arthur Bostrom	Officer Crabtree
John Louis Mansi	Engelbert von Smallhausen
Derek Royle	Monsieur Ernest LeClerc
Trevor T. Smith	German Guard
David Lloyd	German Soldier

The Airmen De-nicked

(Series 6, Episode 5)

With the General away, and fearful of the logical series of revelations that could take place if the airmen are interrogated in Berlin, Gruber suggests that the Resistance may be able to rescue the airmen successfully.

Dramatis Personae

Gorden Kaye	René François Artois
Carmen Silvera	Edith Melba Artois
Vicki Michelle	Yvette Carte-Blanche
Sue Hodge	Mimi Labonq
Richard Marner	Colonel Kurt von Strohm
Gavin Richards	Captain Alberto Bertorelli
Kim Hartman	Private Helga Geerhart
Guy Siner	Lieutenant Hubert Gruber
Kirsten Cooke	Michelle Dubois
Richard Gibson	Herr Otto Flick

Rose Hill	Madame Fanny 'Fifi' Lafanne
John D. Collins	Flt. Lt. Fairfax
Nicholas Frankau	Flt. Lt. Carstairs
Hilary Minster	General von Klinkerhoffen
Kenneth Connor	Monsieur Alfonse
Arthur Bostrom	Officer Crabtree
John Louis Mansi	Engelbert von Smallhausen
Derek Royle	Monsieur Ernest LeClerc
Phoebe Scholfield	Henriette Michelle's Assistant
Trevor T. Smith	German Guard
Howard Leader	German Guard
Ian McLaren	Guard

The Crooked Fences

(Series 6, Episode 6)

Worried with the way things are going, the Colonel, Gruber, Helga - and now Captain Bertorelli too - ask René to find them a fence to sell *The Fallen Madonna*.

Dramatis Personae

Gorden Kaye	René François Artois
Carmen Silvera	Edith Melba Artois
Vicki Michelle	Yvette Carte-Blanche
Sue Hodge	Mimi Labonq
Richard Marner	Colonel Kurt von Strohm
Gavin Richards	Captain Alberto Bertorelli
Kim Hartman	Private Helga Geerhart
Guy Siner	Lieutenant Hubert Gruber
Kirsten Cooke	Michelle Dubois
Richard Gibson	Herr Otto Flick

Rose Hill	Madame Fanny 'Fifi' Lafanne
John D. Collins	Flt. Lt. Fairfax
Nicholas Frankau	Flt. Lt. Carstairs
Hilary Minster	General von Klinkerhoffen
Kenneth Connor	Monsieur Alfonse
Arthur Bostrom	Officer Crabtree
John Louis Mansi	Engelbert von Smallhausen
Derek Royle	Monsieur Ernest LeClerc
Sarah Sherborne	Agent Grace
Iain Mitchell	Priest

Crabtree's Podgeon Pist

(Series 6, Episode 7)

The General threatens to blow up Nouvion if the airmen are not returned to his custody. Meanwhile, Michelle has another crackpot scheme to send them home, and refuses to waiver.

Dramatis Personae

Gorden Kaye	René François Artois
Carmen Silvera	Edith Melba Artois
Vicki Michelle	Yvette Carte-Blanche
Sue Hodge	Mimi Labonq
Richard Marner	Colonel Kurt von Strohm
Gavin Richards	Captain Alberto Bertorelli
Kim Hartman	Private Helga Geerhart
Guy Siner	Lieutenant Hubert Gruber
Kirsten Cooke	Michelle Dubois
Richard Gibson	Herr Otto Flick

Rose Hill	Madame Fanny 'Fifi' Lafanne
John D. Collins	Flt. Lt. Fairfax
Nicholas Frankau	Flt. Lt. Carstairs
Hilary Minster	General von Klinkerhoffen
Kenneth Connor	Monsieur Alfonse
Arthur Bostrom	Officer Crabtree
John Louis Mansi	Engelbert von Smallhausen
Derek Royle	Monsieur Ernest LeClerc
Sarah Sherborne	Agent Grace
Iain Mitchell	Priest

Rising To The Occasion

(Series 6, Episode 8)

With the Colonel, Flick and von Smallhausen held by the Communist Resistance, Gruber calls in von Flockenstuffen to have General von Klinkerhoffen sectioned. Back in the town, Michelle's plan to have the airmen escape by balloon goes awry when helium canisters deploy too early...

Dramatis Personae

Gorden Kaye	René François Artois
Carmen Silvera	Edith Melba Artois
Vicki Michelle	Yvette Carte-Blanche
Sue Hodge	Mimi Labonq
Richard Marner	Colonel Kurt von Strohm
Gavin Richards	Captain Alberto Bertorelli
Kim Hartman	Private Helga Geerhart
Guy Siner	Lieutenant Hubert Gruber
Kirsten Cooke	Michelle Dubois
Richard Gibson	Herr Otto Flick

Rose Hill	Madame Fanny 'Fifi' Lafanne
John D. Collins	Flt. Lt. Fairfax
Nicholas Frankau	Flt. Lt. Carstairs
Hilary Minster	General von Klinkerhoffen
Kenneth Connor	Monsieur Alfonse
Arthur Bostrom	Officer Crabtree
John Louis Mansi	Engelbert von Smallhausen
Derek Royle	Monsieur Ernest LeClerc
Carole Ashby	Louise (Communist Girl)
Phoebe Scholfield	Henriette Michelle's Assistant
Ken Morley	General Von Flockenstuffen
Sarah Sherborne	Agent Grace
Jackie D. Broad	Resistance Girl
Estelle Matthews	Communist Girl

A Quiet Honeymoon

(Series 7, Episode 1)

The newly married LeClercs are shot down, and swiftly arrested by the Colonel. With von Klinkerhoffen hospitalised, Flockenstuffen is making his presence felt at the chateau.

Where exactly is Fanny? The last time she was seen, it was in her bed with 'toy-boy-pensioner-husband' LeClerc, attached to a balloon and heading due south at about 500 feet.

Dramatis Personae

Gorden Kaye	René François Artois
Carmen Silvera	Edith Melba Artois
Vicki Michelle	Yvette Carte-Blanche
Sue Hodge	Mimi Labonq
Richard Marner	Colonel Kurt Von Strohm
Kim Hartman	Private Helga Geerhart
Guy Siner	Lieutenant Hubert Gruber
Kirsten Cooke	Michelle Dubois

Richard Gibson	Herr Otto Flick
Rose Hill	Madame Fanny 'Fifi' Lafanne
John D. Collins	Flt. Lt. Fairfax
Nicholas Frankau	Flt. Lt. Carstairs
Hilary Minster	General Von Klinkerhoffen
Kenneth Connor	Monsieur Alfonse
Arthur Bostrom	Officer Crabtree
John Louis Mansi	Engelbert Von Smallhausen
Robin Parkinson	Monsieur Ernest LeClerc
Ken Morley	General Von Flockenstuffen
Roger Kitter	Captain Alberto Bertorelli
Howard Leader	German Guard
Joyce Windsor	Nurse

An Almighty Bang

(Series 7, Episode 2)

When von Flockenstuffen announces plans for a daring raid to capture Churchill, to be run from the chateau, the Colonel decides it is time to have von Klinkerhoffen reinstated. Meanwhile, back at the Café, the LeClercs are stuck inside a wall...

General von Flockenstuffen decides to launch a lightning raid to capture Churchill. The Colonel, Gruber and Bertorelli resort to desperate measures to prevent this.

Dramatis Personae

Gorden Kaye	René François Artois
Carmen Silvera	Edith Melba Artois
Vicki Michelle	Yvette Carte-Blanche
Sue Hodge	Mimi Labonq
Richard Marner	Colonel Kurt von Strohm
Kim Hartman	Private Helga Geerhart
Guy Siner	Lieutenant Hubert Gruber

Kirsten Cooke	Michelle Dubois
Richard Gibson	Herr Otto Flick
Rose Hill	Madame Fanny 'Fifi' Lafanne
John D. Collins	Flt. Lt. Fairfax
Nicholas Frankau	Flt. Lt. Carstairs
Hilary Minster	General von Klinkerhoffen
Kenneth Connor	Monsieur Alfonse
Arthur Bostrom	Officer Crabtree
John Louis Mansi	Engelbert von Smallhausen
Robin Parkinson	Monsieur Ernest LeClerc
Ken Morley	General von Flockenstuffen
Roger Kitter	Captain Alberto Bertorelli

Fleeing Monks

(Series 7, Episode 3)

As Michelle prepares to send the airmen back to England whilst disguised as Monks, René is attempting to get out of receiving a collaboration medal from the General - an honour for which the Resistance, Communists and townspeople would have him executed!

The Germans plan to give René a medal for collaboration and the Communists plan to shoot him as a traitor. Michelle's plans for smuggling the airmen in the disguise of monks reaches its climax.

Dramatis Personae

Gorden Kaye	René François Artois
Carmen Silvera	Edith Melba Artois
Vicki Michelle	Yvette Carte-Blanche
Sue Hodge	Mimi Labonq
Richard Marner	Colonel Kurt von Strohm
Kim Hartman	Private Helga Geerhart
Guy Siner	Lieutenant Hubert Gruber

Kirsten Cooke	Michelle Dubois
Richard Gibson	Herr Otto Flick
Rose Hill	Madame Fanny 'Fifi' Lafanne
John D. Collins	Flt. Lt. Fairfax
Nicholas Frankau	Flt. Lt. Carstairs
Hilary Minster	General von Klinkerhoffen
Kenneth Connor	Monsieur Alfonse
Arthur Bostrom	Officer Crabtree
John Louis Mansi	Engelbert von Smallhausen
Robin Parkinson	Monsieur Ernest LeClerc
Roger Kitter	Captain Alberto Bertorelli
Roger Hammond	Monk
David Valentine-Webb	Pilot

Up The Crick Without A Piddle

(Series 7, Episode 4)

René and Edith have fled to England in the place of the airmen. They receive medals from Churchill, meet an old friend from the past and sample some of the hardships of war-torn London.

René and Edith arrive safely in England and are shocked to see a familiar face. Freshly honoured by Churchill, they take a look around London before Edith is heads back to Nouvion - and a major cock-up sends René reluctantly with her...

Dramatis Personae

Gorden Kaye	René François Artois
Carmen Silvera	Edith Melba Artois
Vicki Michelle	Yvette Carte-Blanche
Sue Hodge	Mimi Labonq
Richard Marner	Colonel Kurt von Strohm
Kim Hartman	Private Helga Geerhart
Guy Siner	Lieutenant Hubert Gruber
Kirsten Cooke	Michelle Dubois

Richard Gibson	Herr Otto Flick
Rose Hill	Madame Fanny 'Fifi' Lafanne
Sam Kelly	Captain Hans Geering
John D. Collins	Flt. Lt. Fairfax
Nicholas Frankau	Flt. Lt. Carstairs
Hilary Minster	General von Klinkerhoffen
Kenneth Connor	Monsieur Alfonse
Arthur Bostrom	Officer Crabtree
John Louis Mansi	Engelbert von Smallhausen
Robin Parkinson	Monsieur Ernest LeClerc
Roger Kitter	Captain Alberto Bertorelli
Tim Marriott	Tigger Thompson
Eric Dodson	Intelligence Officer
Steve Edwin	Farkington
John James Evans	Churchill
Harriet Thorpe	Ethel

The Gestapo Ruins A Picnic

(Series 7, Episode 5)

General von Klinkerhoffen re-opens the local newspaper as a propaganda sheet with a very reluctant René as its editor. Michelle now plans to build a raft to float the airmen to England.

After discovering a call-to-arms poster in the town square from the Resistance, the General instructs von Klinkerhoffen to reopen Nouvion's newspaper as a propaganda tool - with René installed as puppet editor under Gruber's command.

Dramatis Personae

Gorden Kaye	René François Artois
Carmen Silvera	Edith Melba Artois
Vicki Michelle	Yvette Carte-Blanche
Sue Hodge	Mimi Labonq
Richard Marner	Colonel Kurt von Strohm
Kim Hartman	Private Helga Geerhart
Guy Siner	Lieutenant Hubert Gruber

Kirsten Cooke	Michelle Dubois
Richard Gibson	Herr Otto Flick
Rose Hill	Madame Fanny 'Fifi' Lafanne
John D. Collins	Flt. Lt. Fairfax
Nicholas Frankau	Flt. Lt. Carstairs
Hilary Minster	General von Klinkerhoffen
Kenneth Connor	Monsieur Alfonse
Arthur Bostrom	Officer Crabtree
John Louis Mansi	Engelbert von Smallhausen
Robin Parkinson	Monsieur Ernest LeClerc
Roger Kitter	Captain Alberto Bertorelli
Roger Hammond	Monk

The Spirit Of Nouvion

(Series 7, Episode 6)

With the Resistance running low on funds, Michelle orders René to tunnel into Herr Flick's headquarters and steal the *Fallen Madonna* from his safe. Meanwhile, the newspaper is looking to crown a local woman the 'Spirit of Nouvion'.

The local newspaper, now edited by René, is looking for a woman of strength, beauty and virtue to be the 'Spirit of Nouvion'. Edith applies. Michelle needs René to nick the *Fallen Madonna* to sell it for much needed funds for the Resistance.

Dramatis Personae

Gorden Kaye	René François Artois
Carmen Silvera	Edith Melba Artois
Vicki Michelle	Yvette Carte-Blanche
Sue Hodge	Mimi Labonq
Richard Marner	Colonel Kurt von Strohm
Kim Hartman	Private Helga Geerhart
Guy Siner	Lieutenant Hubert Gruber

Kirsten Cooke	Michelle Dubois
Richard Gibson	Herr Otto Flick
Rose Hill	Madame Fanny 'Fifi' Lafanne
John D. Collins	Flt. Lt. Fairfax
Nichoas Frankau	Flt. Lt. Carstairs
Hilary Minster	General von Klinkerhoffen
Kenneth Connor	Monsieur Alfonse
Arthur Bostrom	Officer Crabtree
John Louis Mansi	Engelbert von Smallhausen
Robin Parkinson	Monsieur Ernest LeClerc
Roger Kitter	Captain Alberto Bertorelli
Lino Omoboni	Italian Soldier

Leg It To Spain!

(Series 7, Episode 7)

As René prepares to escape to Spain with the painting for the rest of the war, the Colonel arrives at the café and seizes the artwork. Meanwhile, Flick and Helga's relationship is up-and-down, and the Germans are determined to achieve a suitable group photo for the paper.

Dramatis Personae

Gorden Kaye	René François Artois
Carmen Silvera	Edith Melba Artois
Vicki Michelle	Yvette Carte-Blanche
Sue Hodge	Mimi Labonq
Richard Marner	Colonel Kurt von Strohm
Kim Hartman	Private Helga Geerhart
Guy Siner	Lieutenant Hubert Gruber
Kirsten Cooke	Michelle Dubois
Richard Gibson	Herr Otto Flick

Rose Hill	Madame Fanny 'Fifi' Lafanne
John D. Collins	Flt. Lt. Fairfax
Nicholas Frankau	Flt. Lt. Carstairs
Hilary Minster	General von Klinkerhoffen
Kenneth Connor	Monsieur Alfonse
Arthur Bostrom	Officer Crabtree
John Louis Mansi	Engelbert von Smallhausen
Robin Parkinson	Monsieur Ernest LeClerc
Roger Kitter	Captain Alberto Bertorelli
Paul Cooper	'London Calling' (Voice)

Prior Engagements

(Series 7, Episode 8)

Following Madame Edith's crowning as the 'Spirit of Nouvion', the General decides that she should marry Captain Bertorelli in order to cement relations between the two sides. A celebration at the chateaux offers Michelle the perfect chance to release the British airmen.

Dramatis Personae

Gorden Kaye	René François Artois
Carmen Silvera	Edith Melba Artois
Vicki Michelle	Yvette Carte-Blanche
Sue Hodge	Mimi Labonq
Richard Marner	Colonel Kurt von Strohm
Kim Hartman	Private Helga Geerhart
Guy Siner	Lieutenant Hubert Gruber
Kirsten Cooke	Michelle Dubois
Richard Gibson	Herr Otto Flick

Rose Hill	Madame Fanny 'Fifi' Lafanne
John D. Collins	Flt. Lt. Fairfax
Nicholas Frankau	Flt. Lt. Carstairs
Hilary Minster	General von Klinkerhoffen
Kenneth Connor	Monsieur Alfonse
Arthur Bostrom	Officer Crabtree
John Louis Mansi	Engelbert von Smallhausen
Robin Parkinson	Monsieur Ernest LeClerc
Roger Kitter	Captain Alberto Bertorelli
Louis Sheldon	German Soldier

Soup And Sausage

(Series 7, Episode 9)

The British airmen get stuck down the drain in the middle of the town square. René must use all his wits to devise unusual ways to feed them and avoid detection by the Germans.

The airmen are now stuck in the sewers directly beneath the town square. It would be quite simple to free them if only the hinges on the access grate weren't rusted solid. As usual, there's a crackpot plan in place - this time involving an ancient ice cream van.

Dramatis Personae

Gorden Kaye	René François Artois
Carmen Silvera	Edith Melba Artois
Vicki Michelle	Yvette Carte-Blanche
Sue Hodge	Mimi Labonq
Richard Marner	Colonel Kurt von Strohm
Kim Hartman	Private Helga Geerhart
Guy Siner	Lieutenant Hubert Gruber

Kirsten Cooke	Michelle Dubois
Richard Gibson	Herr Otto Flick
Rose Hill	Madame Fanny 'Fifi' Lafanne
John D. Collins	Flt. Lt. Fairfax
Nicholas Frankau	Flt. Lt. Carstairs
Hilary Minster	General von Klinkerhoffen
Kenneth Connor	Monsieur Alfonse
Arthur Bostrom	Officer Crabtree
John Louis Mansi	Engelbert von Smallhausen
Robin Parkinson	Monsieur Ernest LeClerc
Roger Kitter	Captain Alberto Bertorelli
Louise Gold	Private Elsa Bigstern

René Of The Gypsies

(Series 7, Episode 10)

The Resistance plan to get the airmen out of the drain in the town square under the cover of a gypsy fair. René and Edith pay a visit to the gypsies where Edith makes a shocking discovery about her childhood.

With ice cream banned throughout Nouvion, Michelle's next attempt to rescue the airmen involves holding a gypsy fair in the town square. Unfortunately, a black cat throws a spanner in the works, and the Resistance are forced to hold the event themselves.

Dramatis Personae

Gorden Kaye	René François Artois
Carmen Silvera	Edith Melba Artois
Vicki Michelle	Yvette Carte-Blanche
Sue Hodge	Mimi Labonq
Richard Marner	Colonel Kurt von Strohm
Kim Hartman	Private Helga Geerhart

Guy Siner	Lieutenant Hubert Gruber
Kirsten Cooke	Michelle Dubois
Richard Gibson	Herr Otto Flick
Rose Hill	Madame Fanny 'Fifi' Lafanne
John D. Collins	Flt. Lt. Fairfax
Nicholas Frankau	Flt. Lt. Carstairs
Hilary Minster	General von Klinkerhoffen
Kenneth Connor	Monsieur Alfonse
Arthur Bostrom	Officer Crabtree
John Louis Mansi	Engelbert von Smallhausen
Robin Parkinson	Monsieur Ernest LeClerc
Roger Kitter	Captain Alberto Bertorelli
Louise Gold	Private Elsa Bigstern
Ruben Lee	Gypsy
Stanley Lebor	Head of the Gypsies
Robert East	Wing Commander Blenkinsop

A Bun In The Oven

(Series 8, Christmas Special)

It is September 13th, 1943; almost 2 years since we last saw René, who is finally -- at long, long last -- rid of the English airmen. His troubles are far from over, however, as Yvette announces her pregnancy. Meanwhile at the chateau, Gruber and the Colonel are growing increasingly worried at the progress of the war.

Dramatis Personae

Gorden Kaye	René François Artois
Carmen Silvera	Edith Melba Artois
Vicki Michelle	Yvette Carte-Blanche
Sue Hodge	Mimi Labonq
Richard Marner	Colonel Kurt von Strohm
Kim Hartman	Private Helga Geerhart
Guy Siner	Lieutenant Hubert Gruber
Kirsten Cooke	Michelle Dubois

Richard Gibson	Herr Otto Flick
Rose Hill	Madame Fanny 'Fifi' Lafanne
Hilary Minster	General von Klinkerhoffen
Kenneth Connor	Monsieur Alfonse
Arthur Bostrom	Officer Crabtree
John Louis Mansi	Engelbert von Smallhausen
Robin Parkinson	Monsieur Ernest LeClerc
Paul Cooper	'London Calling' (Voice)
Michael Cotterill	The Pope

Arousing Suspicions

(Series 8, Episode 1)

When Michelle devises plans for a radio station, getting the necessary equipment is only the beginning of the problem - particularly when key components end up in the chateau.

Dramatis Personae

Gorden Kaye	René François Artois
Carmen Silvera	Edith Melba Artois
Vicki Michelle	Yvette Carte-Blanche
Sue Hodge	Mimi Labonq
Richard Marner	Colonel Kurt von Strohm
Kim Hartman	Private Helga Geerhart
Guy Siner	Lieutenant Hubert Gruber
Kirsten Cooke	Michelle Dubois
Richard Gibson	Herr Otto Flick
Rose Hill	Madame Fanny 'Fifi' Lafanne

Hilary Minster	General Von Klinkerhoffen
Kenneth Connor	Monsieur Alfonse
Arthur Bostrom	Officer Crabtree
John Louis Mansi	Engelbert von Smallhausen
Robin Parkinson	Monsieur Ernest LeClerc
Paul Cooper	'London Calling' (Voice)
Kate Kenny	Major
Marek Anton	German Soldier

A Woman Never Lies

Series 8, Episode 2

Following the commotion at the chateau, the Resistance are blackmailing Helga, Gruber and the Colonel with evidence of *The Fallen Madonna*. The only chance they have of raising the ten million franc ransom is to hold-up the garrison pay truck! Meanwhile, Michelle's radio station is beginning to take shape.

Dramatis Personae

Gorden Kaye	René François Artois
Carmen Silvera	Edith Melba Artois
Vicki Michelle	Yvette Carte-Blanche
Sue Hodge	Mimi Labonq
Richard Marner	Colonel Kurt von Strohm
Kim Hartman	Private Helga Geerhart
Guy Siner	Lieutenant Hubert Gruber
Kirsten Cooke	Michelle Dubois

Richard Gibson	Herr Otto Flick
Rose Hill	Madame Fanny 'Fifi' Lafanne
Hilary Minster	General von Klinkerhoffen
Kenneth Connor	Monsieur Alfonse
Arthur Bostrom	Officer Crabtree
John Louis Mansi	Engelbert von Smallhausen
Robin Parkinson	Monsieur Ernest LeClerc
Geoff Garratt	Juan Garcia
Huw Tipler	Guard
David Taylor	Guard

Hitler's Last Heil

(Series 8, Episode 3)

It's René's birthday, and Edith has a big surprise for her loving husband - she's bought him a car! At the chateau, Hitler and Goering (or rather, their doubles) are due, and the Resistance are bound to make an attempt on their lives...

Dramatis Personae

Gorden Kaye	René François Artois
Carmen Silvera	Edith Melba Artois
Vicki Michelle	Yvette Carte-Blanche
Sue Hodge	Mimi Labonq
Richard Marner	Colonel Kurt von Strohm
Kim Hartman	Private Helga Geerhart
Guy Siner	Lieutenant Hubert Gruber
Kirsten Cooke	Michelle Dubois
Richard Gibson	Herr Otto Flick
Rose Hill	Madame Fanny 'Fifi' Lafanne

Hilary Minster	General von Klinkerhoffen
Kenneth Connor	Monsieur Alfonse
Arthur Bostrom	Officer Crabtree
John Louis Mansi	Engelbert von Smallhausen
Robin Parkinson	Monsieur Ernest LeClerc
David Rowlands	Doctor LeCount
Michael Jayes	Priest
David Janson	'Hitler'
Michael Sheard	'Goering'
John Hoye	Guard
Jonathan Gleeson	Guard
Julian Moss	Guard
Kit Hillier	Guard
Samantha O'Brien	Kitchen Girl

Awful Wedded Wife

(Series 8, Episode 4)

Amidst the fall-out from the failed radio station launch, René is forced to pay out almost 67,000 francs of the café's takings. Flick and von Smallhausen are still imprisoned, and Gruber and the Colonel are forced to impersonate Hitler and Goering once more. Meanwhile, something curious is taking place at the church.

Dramatis Personae

Gorden Kaye	René François Artois
Carmen Silvera	Edith Melba Artois
Vicki Michelle	Yvette Carte-Blanche
Sue Hodge	Mimi Labonq
Richard Marner	Colonel Kurt von Strohm
Kim Hartman	Private Helga Geerhart
Guy Siner	Lieutenant Hubert Gruber
Kirsten Cooke	Michelle Dubois
Richard Gibson	Herr Otto Flick

Rose Hill	Madame Fanny 'Fifi' Lafanne
Hilary Minster	General von Klinkerhoffen
Kenneth Connor	Monsieur Alfonse
Arthur Bostrom	Officer Crabtree
John Louis Mansi	Engelbert von Smallhausen
Robin Parkinson	Monsieur Ernest LeClerc
Carole Ashby	Louise (Communist Girl)
Michael Jayes	Priest
Annabel Lambe	Agnette
Paul David Betts	Guard
James Bingham	Guard
Elizabeth Ash	Maxine (Communist Girl)
Sarah Hauenstein	Communist Resistance Girl

Firing Squashed

(Series 8, Episode 5)

Whilst Flick and von Smallhausen look set to face the firing squad for robbing the garrison pay truck, the Colonel and Lieutenant Gruber - still dressed as Hitler and Goering - are captured by the Communists. Michelle's Resistance wish to use the duo for their own ends, but who will win?

Dramatis Personae

Gorden Kaye	René François Artois
Carmen Silvera	Edith Melba Artois
Vicki Michelle	Yvette Carte-Blanche
Sue Hodge	Mimi Labonq
Richard Marner	Colonel Kurt von Strohm
Kim Hartman	Private Helga Geerhart
Guy Siner	Lieutenant Hubert Gruber
Kirsten Cooke	Michelle Dubois
Richard Gibson	Herr Otto Flick

Rose Hill	Madame Fanny 'Fifi' Lafanne
Hilary Minster	General von Klinkerhoffen
Kenneth Connor	Monsieur Alfonse
Arthur Bostrom	Officer Crabtree
John Louis Mansi	Engelbert von Smallhausen
Robin Parkinson	Monsieur Ernest LeClerc
Carole Ashby	Louise (Communist Girl)
Elizabeth Ash	Maxine (Communist Girl)
Christine Moore	Desiree
Amanda Gibson-Lees	Communist Resistance Girl
Tim Faulkner	Soldier
Friedrich Solms-Baruth	Soldier

A Fishful Of Francs

(Series 8, Episode 6)

As the Colonel attempts to pay off the Resistance with ten million francs concealed in a large dogfish, Herr Flick and Monsieur Alfonse get in the way. At the café, General von Klinkerhoffen forces René and Madame Edith into the Hitler and Goering uniforms, and it looks like they're bomb fodder.

Dramatis Personae

Gorden Kaye	René François Artois
Carmen Silvera	Edith Melba Artois
Vicki Michelle	Yvette Carte-Blanche
Sue Hodge	Mimi Labonq
Richard Marner	Colonel Kurt von Strohm
Kim Hartman	Private Helga Geerhart
Guy Siner	Lieutenant Hubert Gruber
Kirsten Cooke	Michelle Dubois
Richard Gibson	Herr Otto Flick

Rose Hill	Madame Fanny 'Fifi' Lafanne
Hilary Minster	General Von Klinkerhoffen
Kenneth Connor	Monsieur Alfonse
Arthur Bostrom	Officer Crabtree
John Louis Mansi	Engelbert von Smallhausen
Robin Parkinson	Monsieur Ernest LeClerc
Carole Ashby	Louise (Communist Girl)
Elizabeth Ash	Maxine (Communist Girl)
Jack Hedley	General Von Karzibrot
Mark Carey	Soldier
David Hopkins	Soldier

Swan Song

(Series 8, Episode 7)

Believing René and Edith to be dead by firing squad, Madame Fanny and LeClerc empty the till and head to Paris for one last binge. Back in Nouvion, the Resistance take over the running of the café, whilst Gruber and the Colonel plan to escape to Spain to sell the painting.

Dramatis Personae

Gorden Kaye	René François Artois
Carmen Silvera	Edith Melba Artois
Vicki Michelle	Yvette Carte-Blanche
Sue Hodge	Mimi Labonq
Richard Marner	Colonel Kurt von Strohm
Kim Hartman	Private Helga Geerhart
Guy Siner	Lieutenant Hubert Gruber
Kirsten Cooke	Michelle Dubois
Richard Gibson	Herr Otto Flick

Rose Hill	Madame Fanny 'Fifi' Lafanne
Hilary Minster	General von Klinkerhoffen
Kenneth Connor	Monsieur Alfonse
Arthur Bostrom	Officer Crabtree
John Louis Mansi	Engelbert von Smallhausen
Robin Parkinson	Monsieur Ernest LeClerc
David Rowlands	Doctor LeCount
Jack Hedley	General Von Karzibrot
Miles Richardson	Captain Frobisher
Darren Matthews	Pilkers
Brian Weston	Soldier

Gone With The Windmill

(Series 9, Episode 1)

Having been double-crossed by Herr Flick, Gruber and the Colonel are looking for a way to 'un-desert'. Madame Edith concocts a plot that will appear that they have been kidnapped. Unfortunately, the General fails to take the hint and René is forced to save the duo before they are blown up...

Dramatis Personae

Gorden Kaye	René François Artois
Carmen Silvera	Edith Melba Artois
Vicki Michelle	Yvette Carte-Blanche
Sue Hodge	Mimi Labonq
Richard Marner	Colonel Kurt von Strohm
Kim Hartman	Private Helga Geerhart
Guy Siner	Lieutenant Hubert Gruber
Kirsten Cooke	Michelle Dubois
Rose Hill	Madame Fanny 'Fifi' Lafanne

Hilary Minster	General Von Klinkerhoffen
Kenneth Connor	Monsieur Alfonse
Arthur Bostrom	Officer Crabtree
John Louis Mansi	Engelbert von Smallhausen
Robin Parkinson	Monsieur Ernest LeClerc
David Janson	Herr Otto Flick
Carole Ashby	Louise (Communist Girl)
Sarah Hauenstein	Communist Resistance Girl
Peter Clapham	Field Marshall
Jeremy Lloyd	Wolfgang
Taryn Dielle	Tart
Natalie Tomlinson	Tart
Jeremy Beckman	Soldier

A Tour De France

(Series 9, Episode 2)

René is being held hostage as Louise's love slave, and is missing presumed exploded by the Nazis. The Resistance, and the girls at the café plan tributes to their fallen hero; René is desperate to escape being shared around by the Communists in their underground bunker!

Dramatis Personae

Gorden Kaye	René François Artois
Carmen Silvera	Edith Melba Artois
Vicki Michelle	Yvette Carte-Blanche
Sue Hodge	Mimi Labonq
Richard Marner	Colonel Kurt von Strohm
Kim Hartman	Private Helga Geerhart
Guy Siner	Lieutenant Hubert Gruber
Kirsten Cooke	Michelle Dubois
Rose Hill	Madame Fanny 'Fifi' Lafanne

Hilary Minster	General Von Klinkerhoffen
Kenneth Connor	Monsieur Alfonse
Arthur Bostrom	Officer Crabtree
John Louis Mansi	Engelbert von Smallhausen
Robin Parkinson	Monsieur Ernest LeClerc
David Janson	Herr Otto Flick
Carole Ashby	Louise (Communist Girl)
Sarah Hauenstein	Communist Resistance Girl
Ann Michelle	Communist Girl
Cheryl Fergison	Desiree (Communist Girl)
Linda Styan	Nola (Communist Girl)
Debi Thomson	Claudette (Communist Girl)

Dead Man Marching

Series 9, Episode 3

Still believing René to be deceased, Nouvion puts on a procession of their hero's boots and beret. The man himself, meanwhile, is forced to hide in the local museum until he can be smuggled away to England.

Dramatis Personae

Gorden Kaye	René François Artois
Carmen Silvera	Edith Melba Artois
Vicki Michelle	Yvette Carte-Blanche
Sue Hodge	Mimi Labonq
Richard Marner	Colonel Kurt von Strohm
Kim Hartman	Private Helga Geerhart
Guy Siner	Lieutenant Hubert Gruber
Kirsten Cooke	Michelle Dubois
Rose Hill	Madame Fanny 'Fifi' Lafanne

Hilary Minster	General von Klinkerhoffen
Kenneth Connor	Monsieur Alfonse
Arthur Bostrom	Officer Crabtree
John Louis Mansi	Engelbert von Smallhausen
Robin Parkinson	Monsieur Ernest LeClerc
David Janson	Herr Otto Flick
David Rowlands	Doctor LeCount
Max Diamond	Peasant
Peter Dukes	Peasant
Jon Hurn	Peasant
Nancy Olive Moore	Cleaning Lady

Tarts and Flickers

(Series 9, Episode 4)

As Michelle struggles to send a microfilm to England by homing pigeon, Herr Flick captures Yvette and Mimi in order to gain access to the café and search for *The Fallen Madonna with the Big Boobies*. A mistaken rendezvous in a broom cupboard leaves Edith and René equally flustered!

Dramatis Personae

Gorden Kaye	René François Artois
Carmen Silvera	Edith Melba Artois
Vicki Michelle	Yvette Carte-Blanche
Sue Hodge	Mimi Labonq
Richard Marner	Colonel Kurt von Strohm
Kim Hartman	Private Helga Geerhart
Guy Siner	Lieutenant Hubert Gruber
Kirsten Cooke	Michelle Dubois
Rose Hill	Madame Fanny 'Fifi' Lafanne

Hilary Minster	General Von Klinkerhoffen
Kenneth Connor	Monsieur Alfonse
Arthur Bostrom	Officer Crabtree
John Louis Mansi	Engelbert von Smallhausen
Robin Parkinson	Monsieur Ernest LeClerc
David Janson	Herr Otto Flick
Paul Cooper	'London Calling' (Voice)
Paul David Betts	German Soldier
Peter Dayson	German Soldier
Paul Cooper	Churchill (Voice)

A Fishy Sendoff

(Series 9, Episode 5)

It's the annual fishmonger's parade to the coast, and Michelle has a plan to enter a float capable of spiriting a group across the channel and to freedom in England. Meanwhile, General von Klinkerhoffen has finalised his plans to blow up Hitler and requires Gruber and the Colonel's assistance.

Dramatis Personae

Gorden Kaye	René François Artois
Carmen Silvera	Edith Melba Artois
Vicki Michelle	Yvette Carte-Blanche
Sue Hodge	Mimi Labonq
Richard Marner	Colonel Kurt von Strohm
Kim Hartman	Private Helga Geerhart
Guy Siner	Lieutenant Hubert Gruber
Kirsten Cooke	Michelle Dubois
Rose Hill	Madame Fanny 'Fifi' Lafanne

Hilary Minster	General von Klinkerhoffen
Kenneth Connor	Monsieur Alfonse
Arthur Bostrom	Officer Crabtree
John Louis Mansi	Engelbert von Smallhausen
Robin Parkinson	Monsieur Ernest LeClerc
David Janson	Herr Otto Flick
Matthew Woolcott	Soldier at Station
David Hopkins	German Officer
Ian Soundy	Sentry
James Pertwee	Soldier on Coast
Dennis Arnell	Onlooker

A Winkle In Time

(Series 9, Episode 6)

The invasion has started. Nouvion's liberation can be no more than hours away; the Germans are retreating, the girls in the café are practicing their jive -- and the British airmen are back!

Dramatis Personae

Gorden Kaye	René François Artois
Carmen Silvera	Edith Melba Artois
Vicki Michelle	Yvette Carte-Blanche
Sue Hodge	Mimi Labonq
Richard Marner	Colonel Kurt von Strohm
Kim Hartman	Private Helga Geerhart
Guy Siner	Lieutenant Hubert Gruber
Kirsten Cooke	Michelle Dubois
Rose Hill	Madame Fanny 'Fifi' Lafanne
John D. Collins	Flt. Lt. Fairfax
Nicholas Frankau	Flt. Lt. Carstairs

Hilary Minster	General von Klinkerhoffen
Kenneth Connor	Monsieur Alfonse
Arthur Bostrom	Officer Crabtree
John Louis Mansi	Engelbert von Smallhausen
Robin Parkinson	Monsieur Ernest LeClerc
David Janson	Herr Otto Flick
Paul Cooper	'London Calling' (Voice)
Giles Watling	Major Twistleton-Smythe
James Barron	Captain Starkington

The Return of 'Allo 'Allo

2007: One-off Special Episode

Written by Jeremy Lloyd

René is writing his memoirs and needs help to fill in the "big gaps". Features some of the original cast reprising their roles; inter-worked with a documentary about the show's history.

Dramatis Personae

Gorden Kaye	René François Artois
Vicki Michelle	Yvette Carte-Blanche
Sue Hodge	Mimi Labonq
Guy Siner	Lieutenant Hubert Gruber
Kirsten Cooke	Michelle Dubois
John D. Collins	Flt. Lt. Fairfax
Nicholas Frankau	Flt. Lt. Carstairs
Arthur Bostrom	Officer Crabtree
Robin Parkinson	Monsieur Ernest LeClerc

ACKNOWLEDGEMENTS:

MERCI D. C. , MERCI D, C.

David Conville OBE

Imagine! Were it not for the initials 'D.C.', Mimi Labonq might never have been born. You might also think it was something of a coincidence that these initials happened not only once, but twice in the build-up to the character being created. Therefore, Mimi would firstly like to thank David Conville, who formed The New Shakespeare Company at the Open Air Theatre, Regents Park, in 1962. He was both Chairman and Artistic Director. David Conville cast Mimi as part of his season in 1986.

David Croft OBE

One evening in August the second 'D. C.' appeared, when David Croft attended a performance of *A Midsummer Night's Dream* and discovered in Peaseblossom a future Mimi Labonq, his inspired creation in *'Allo 'Allo.*

David Croft wrote Sue into the show in 1987. It is with fond memories and deepest gratitude that Mimi holds the second D.C.'s heart almost as close to her as the irresistible René's.

Keith 'Paddington' Richards

Mimi would personally like to acknowledge and thank the gifted musical director Keith Richards, affectionately known in the industry as 'Paddington', for his musical arrangements and direction in the live show *'Allo 'Allo Again 'Mimi and Me'* and for illustrating this book.

Roberta Kanal Agent

Special thanks go to the London Agent Roberta Kanal who has looked after Mimi and everything pertaining to *'Allo 'Allo* for the last 30 years and continues to do so.

'ALLO 'ALLO AGAIN

MIMI & ME: THE STAGE SHOW

On the 14th December 1992, it was all over as the final episode of *'Allo 'Allo'* entitled *A Winkle in Time,* was watched by millions of adoring fans who said 'Adieu, Adieu' to Café René. -- UNTIL NOW!

With great pleasure and by popular demand, we bring you Mimi Labonq, the Pocket Dynamo, that 4ft 11 inch bundle of fun, in her very own special show *'Allo 'Allo Again: Mimi & Me.*

'Allo 'Allo Again: Mimi & Me offers a visual feast of laughter and music, with Mimi and her Musical Director Keith 'Paddington' Richards at the piano, as Mimi reveals behind-the-scenes antics of the worldwide popular TV series *'Allo 'Allo,* from the golden days of comedy. Add in a splash of witty music and hilarious visuals and you have a unique show filled with memories and first class entertainment.

Audiences are invited to 'Mimi's Q and A' time. Mimi will also be available for a meet-and-greet to sign photographs and copies of her book and DVD.

A unique luncheon or intimate café style presentation with an option to include afternoon tea, cheese & wine, dinner or an intimate theatre evening for your loving comedy audience will be on offer. Cruises or cabaret in your hotel or restaurant provide a unique event for all your guests. Whatever the occasion or event this is certainly something you would not want to miss.

For further information and bookings, contact:

Chris Gidney
chris@thatsentertainmentproductions.co.uk

Keith 'Paddington' Richards   Sue Hodge